Music in primitive culture

Music in
Primitive
Culture

by Bruno Nettl

HARVARD UNIVERSITY PRESS
Cambridge

Second Printing, 1969

Distributed in Great Britain by
Oxford University Press
London

Library of Congress Catalog Card Number 56–8551
SBN 674–59000–7
Printed in the United States of America

To my father

Preface

The purpose of this book is to introduce the music of primitive people to students, scholars, and laymen. It is not intended to interest the specialist in non-Western music, who will find little here that is new to him. The material presented is based on works already published and on facts already known; hence the nature of the book is truly introductory, and no attempt has been made to draw up a set of definitive conclusions. I have not covered systematically the music of all primitive cultures: this would be impossible at present even if time and space were available, because of lack of source materials. It has been my purpose, rather, to show the kinds of phenomena that occur in primitive music, to give examples, and to indicate how they have been studied and to what *general* conclusions they have led. For the student who wishes to continue the study of primitive music in more detail, Chapter 3 discusses methods of analysis and research, and the annotated bibliography supplies further literature.

Primitive music is a subject bordering on several disciplines: musicology, anthropology, folklore, psychology, and others; and a student in this field has almost inevitably been trained in one of those areas. Thus it comes about that, in any book on primitive music, the basic disciplinary bias of the writer is evident. I am myself a musicologist, and do not pretend to approach the subject from other points of view. I have tried to include the necessary anthropological, folkloristic, and other data and theory; but the anthropologist or folklorist who reads this may find that the interests of a musicologist in primitive music are not always the same as his. The distribution of emphasis was decided partly by this basic disciplinary bias; it was also guided by what has been stressed or neglected in previous research, since this book is a survey of the work that has been done in the past and a summary of the theories that have been formulated.

Some of the examples of primitive music have been taken from printed sources, and the rest I have transcribed from my own and other collections of recordings. Usually the examples have been limited to the illustration of specific points, with aspects that do not contribute to the illustration omitted. The texts of vocal music have not been included where they do not so contribute, for transcription of texts from recordings is almost impossible even if the language is known, and the examples in this book cover over thirty languages.

It would be very difficult to mention all the teachers, colleagues, and friends who have indirectly assisted in making this book by formal and informal instruction and discussion. My thanks are extended to them all. I am most indebted, however, to Dr. George Herzog, who introduced me to the study of primitive music, trained me in the fundamentals of the field, and taught me most of what I know about it.

BRUNO NETTL

July 1955

Contents

List of Examples of Primitive Music

(following page 183)

1. *Shona Karanga (northern Rhodesia) song from a tale*
   Transcribed by Bruno Nettl; recorded by the University of California African Expedition, 1948; deposited at Indiana University.

2. *Kouyou (French Equatorial Africa) women's dance song*
   Transcribed by Bruno Nettl from the Ethnic Folkways Library album "Music of Equatorial Africa." Used by permission of Folkways Records and Service Corp.

3. *Arapaho Peyote song*
   Transcribed by B. Nettl; recorded by B. Nettl, 1952; deposited at Indiana University.

4. *Arapaho Peyote song*
   Transcribed by B. Nettl; recorded by B. Nettl, 1952; deposited at Indiana University.

5. *Two Shawnee Peyote songs*
   Transcribed by B. Nettl; recorded by B. Nettl, 1952; deposited at Indiana University.

6. *Shawnee turkey song*
   Transcribed by B. Nettl; recorded by C. F. and E. W. Voegelin, 1932; deposited at Indiana University. Reprinted from *Southwestern Journal of Anthropology*, 9:280 (1953), by permission of the editor of the journal.

7. *Modoc (southern Oregon) song*

   Transcribed by Jody C. Hall; recorded by Leslie Spier; deposited at Indiana University. Used by permission of Mr. Spier.

8. *Cheremis children's song*

   Quoted in V. M. Vasiliev, *Pesni naroda mari* (Folk songs of the Cheremis) (Kazan, 1919), no. 3.

9. *Songs with ditonic scales*

   (a) Shawnee. Transcribed by B. Nettl; recorded by C. F. and E. W. Voegelin; deposited at Indiana University. Reprinted from *Southwestern Journal of Anthropology*, 9:280 (1953), by permission of the editor of the journal.

   (b) Vedda. Quoted in Max Wertheimer, "Musik der Wedda," *Sämmelbande der internationalen Musikgesellschaft*, 10:304 (1909). Used by permission of the publisher, Breitkopf and Härtel, Wiesbaden.

   (c) Botocudo. Quoted in Curt Sachs, *The Rise of Music in the Ancient World, East and West* (New York, 1943), p. 32. Used by permission of the publisher, W. W. Norton & Company, Inc.

10. *Menomini (Wisconsin) song, with its scale*

    Song no. 113 in Frances Densmore, *Menominee Music*, Bulletin 102 of the Bureau of American Ethnology (Washington, 1932). Used by permission of the Bureau of American Ethnology, Smithsonian Institution.

11. *Uitoto song (fragment), with its scale*

    Example 32 in Fritz Bose, "Die Musik der Uitoto," *Zeitschrift für vergleichende Musikwissenschaft*, 2:1–40 (1934).

12. *Pawnee Ghost Dance song, with its scale*

    Song no. 58 in Frances Densmore, *Pawnee Music*, Bulletin 93 of the Bureau of American Ethnology (Washington, 1929). Used by permission of the Bureau of American Ethnology, Smithsonian Institution.

13. *Arapaho Round Dance song*

    Transcribed by B. Nettl; recorded by Z. Salzmann, 1948; deposited at Indiana University.

14. *Cheremis song*

   Song no. 208 in Robert Lach, *Tscheremissische Gesänge* (Abt. 3 of Vol. 1 of *Gesänge Russischer Kriegsgefangener*; Vienna, 1918–1952). Used by permission of the publisher, the Vienna Academy of Sciences.

15. *Arapaho Peyote song*

   Transcribed by B. Nettl; recorded by Z. Salzmann, 1948; deposited at Indiana University.

16. *Taos Pueblo (New Mexico) song (fragment)*

   Song no. 6 in George Herzog, "A Comparison of Pueblo and Pima Musical Styles," *Journal of American Folklore*, 49:283–417 (1938). Used by permission of the American Folklore Society.

17. *Duma Karanga (southern Rhodesia) song for musical bow*

   Transcribed by B. Nettl; recorded by the University of California African Expedition, 1948; deposited at Indiana University.

18. *Papago (Arizona) flute song*

   Quoted in Frances Densmore, *Papago Music*, Bulletin 90 of the Bureau of American Ethnology (Washington, 1929), p. 217. Used by permission of the Bureau of American Ethnology, Smithsonian Institution.

19. *Georgian (Caucasus) song*

   Song no. 235 in Robert Lach, *Georgische Gesänge* (Abt. 1 of Vol. 3 of *Gesänge Russischer Kriegsgefangener*; Vienna, 1918–1952). Used by permission of the publisher, the Vienna Academy of Sciences.

20. *Ibo (Nigeria) war song (fragment)*

   Transcribed by B. Nettl; recorded by B. Nettl, 1950; deposited at Indiana University.

21. *Makah (Washington) song*

   Quoted in Frances Densmore, *Nootka and Quileute Music*, Bulletin 124 of the Bureau of American Ethnology (Washington, 1939), p. 101. Used by permission of the Bureau of American Ethnology, Smithsonian Institution.

22. *Arapaho Peyote song*

    Transcribed by B. Nettl; recorded by Z. Salzmann, 1948; deposited at Indiana University.

23. *Cheremis song*

    Song no. 27 in Robert Lach, *Tscheremissische Gesänge* (Abt. 3 of Vol. 1 of *Gesänge Russischer Kriegsgefangener*; Vienna, 1918–1952). Used by permission of the publisher, the Vienna Academy of Sciences.

24. *Bemba (Rhodesia), music for four drums (fragment)*

    Quoted in Curt Sachs, *Rhythm and Tempo* (New York, 1953), p. 42. Used by permission of the publisher, W. W. Norton & Company, Inc.

25. *Iroquois (New York) Eagle Dance song*

    Quoted in Gertrude P. Kurath, "Local Diversity in Iroquois Music and Dance" in *Symposium on Local Diversity in Iroquois Culture*, edited by William N. Fenton, Bulletin 149 of the Bureau of American Ethnology (Washington, 1951), p. 124. Used by permission of the Bureau of American Ethnology, Smithsonian Institution.

26. *Arapaho Ghost Dance song*

    Quoted in James Mooney, *The Ghost-Dance Religion and the Sioux Outbreak of 1890*, Annual Report No. 14 of the Bureau of American Ethnology, part 2 (Washington, 1896), p. 1006. Used by permission of the Bureau of American Ethnology, Smithsonian Institution.

27. *Buriat Mongol song*

    Song no. 1 in Ernst Emsheimer and others, *The Music of the Mongols* (Stockholm, 1943). Used by permission of the author.

28. *Ibo (Nigeria) children's dance song*

    Transcribed by B. Nettl; recorded by B. Nettl, 1950; deposited at Indiana University.

29. *Arapaho song*

    Transcribed by B. Nettl; recorded by Z. Salzmann, 1948; deposited at Indiana University.

30. *Arapaho Peyote song*

> Transcribed by B. Nettl; recorded by Z. Salzmann, 1948; deposited at Indiana University.

31. *Tsimshian (Alaska) song, with its motifs (fragment)*

> Song no. 5 in Viola E. Garfield, Paul S. Wingert, and Marius Barbeau, *The Tsimshian: their Arts and Music,* Publication of the American Ethnological Society no. 18 (New York, 1951). Used by permission of the American Ethnological Society.

32. *Padleirmiut Eskimo*

> Song no. 6 in Zygmunt Estreicher, "Die Musik der Eskimos," *Anthropos,* 45:716 (1950). Used by permission of the publisher, Anthropos-Institute, Fribourg.

33. *Mordwin (Finno-Ugric tribe, Russia) song*

> Taken from song no. 47 in Robert Lach, *Mordwinische Gesänge* (Abt. 2 of Vol. 1 of *Gesänge Russischer Kriegsgefangener;* Vienna, 1918–1952). Used by permission of the publisher, the Vienna Academy of Sciences.

34. *Cheremis song*

> Song no. 9 in Robert Lach, *Tscheremissische Gesänge* (Abt. 3 of Vol. 1 of *Gesänge Russischer Kriegsgefangener;* Vienna, 1918–1952). (Same source.)

35. *Song from Equatorial Africa (tribe unknown; fragment)*

> Transcribed by B. Nettl from the Ethnic Folkways Library album "Music of Equatorial Africa." Used by permission of Folkways Records and Service Corp.

36. *Shawnee antiphonal song (fragment)*

> Transcribed by B. Nettl; recorded by B. Nettl, 1952; deposited at Indiana University.

37. *Equatorial African song for voices and musical bow (fragment)*

> Transcribed by B. Nettl from the Ethnic Folkways Library album "Music of Equatorial Africa." Used by permission of Folkways Records and Service Corp.

38. *Shona Karanga (northern Rhodesia) song*

    Transcribed by B. Nettl; recorded by the University of California African Expedition, 1948; deposited at Indiana University.

39. *Tonga (northern Rhodesia) song for voices and musical bow*

    Transcribed by B. Nettl; recorded by the University of California African Expedition, 1948; deposited at Indiana University.

40. *Gur (tribe west of the Caspian Sea) song*

    Song no. 311 in Robert Lach, *Georgische Gesänge* (Abt. 1 of Vol. 3 of *Gesänge Russischer Kriegsgefangener*; Vienna, 1918–1952). Used by permission of the publisher, the Vienna Academy of Sciences.

41. *Caroline Islands song*

    Song no. 77 in George Herzog, *Die Musik der Karolinen-Inseln*, Thilenius, *Ergebnisse der Südsee-Expedition* 1908–10, II. Ethnographie: B. Mikronesien, Bd. 9, Eilers, Westkarolinen, II. Halbband (Hamburg, 1936), p. 320. Used by permission of the publisher, Cram, de Gruyter, and Co.

42. *Belgian Congo song (fragment)*

    Transcribed by B. Nettl from the Denis-Roosevelt Expedition album "The Belgian Congo Records." Used by permission of Reeves Sound Studios, Inc., which recorded the album.

43. *Caroline Islands song (fragment)*

    Song no. 53 in George Herzog, *Die Musik der Karolinen-Inseln*, Thilenius, *Ergebnisse der Südsee-Expedition* 1908–10, II. Ethnographie: B. Mikronesien, Bd. 9, Eilers, Westkarolinen, II. Halbband (Hamburg, 1936), p. 309. Used by permission of the publisher, Cram, de Gruyter, and Co.

44. *Arapaho song (fragment)*

    Transcribed by B. Nettl; recorded by Z. Salzmann, 1948; deposited at Indiana University.

45. *Moni (Malacca) song (fragment)*

From M. Kolinski, quoted by Curt Sachs in *The Rise of Music in the Ancient World, East and West* (New York, 1943), p. 51. Used by permission of the publisher, W. W. Norton & Company, Inc.

46. *Uvea (Polynesia) song (fragment)*

Quoted in Edwin G. Burrows, *Songs of Uvea and Futuna*, Bishop Museum Bulletin 183 (1945), p. 9. Used by permission of the editors of the bulletin.

47. *Equatorial African song (fragment)*

Transcribed by B. Nettl from the Ethnic Folkways Library album "Music of Equatorial Africa." Used by permission of Folkways Records and Service Corp.

48. *Shona Karanga music for sansa orchestra and voices*

Transcribed by B. Nettl; recorded by the University of California African Expedition, 1948; deposited at Indiana University.

49. *South African song for musical bow (fragment)*

Transcribed by B. Nettl; recorded by the University of California African Expedition, 1948; deposited at Indiana University.

50. *Thompson River Indians (British Columbia) song*

Song no. 12 in Otto Abraham and E. M. von Hornbostel, "Phonographierte Indianermelodien aus Britisch Columbia" in *Boas Anniversary Volume* (New York, 1906). Used by permission of Stechert-Hafner, Inc., owner of the copyright.

51. *Paiute song*

Song no. 5 in George Herzog, "Plains Ghost Dance and Great Basin Music," *American Anthropologist,* 37:403–419. Used by permission of the American Anthropological Association, publisher of the journal.

52. *Yuma (Arizona) song*

Song no. 17 in George Herzog, "The Yuman Musical Style," *Journal of American Folklore,* 41:183–231. Used by permission of the American Folklore Society.

53. *Navaho Gambling song*

Quoted in George Herzog, "Speech-Melody and Primitive Music," *Musical Quarterly*, 20:452–466 (1934). Used by permission of the editors of *Musical Quarterly*.

54. *Choctaw (Mississippi) song*

Song no. 41 in Frances Densmore, *Choctaw Music*, Anthropological Papers, no. 28, from Bulletin 136 of the Bureau of American Ethnology (Washington, 1943). Used by permission of the Bureau of American Ethnology, Smithsonian Institution.

55. *Ibo (Nigeria) version of "Frère Jacques" (fragment)*

Transcribed by B. Nettl; recorded by B. Nettl, 1950; deposited at Indiana University.

56. *Soleil Malade, Haitian Negro song*

Transcribed by B. Nettl from "Haiti Folk Songs," general record 5004B. Used by permission of Folkways Records and Service Corp.

57. *Haitian drum rhythms from two Vodun cults*

Quoted in Harold Courlander, *Haiti Singing* (Chapel Hill, 1939), pp. 179–180. Used by permission of the author.

58. *Hallie Rock, spiritual (Bahamas)*

Transcribed by B. Nettl from recording in the Archive of American Folk Song, Library of Congress.

59. *Round the Bay of Mexico (Bahamas; fragment)*

Transcribed by B. Nettl from recording in the Archive of American Folk Song, Library of Congress.

60. *Another Man Done Gone (Alabama)*

Transcribed by B. Nettl from recording in the Archive of American Folk Song, Library of Congress.

*Music in
primitive
culture*

1

Introduction

In many parts of the world today there are people who are conventionally called primitive. They have simple cultures with no system of reading and writing of their own, although they usually possess some kind of tribal organization. It is their music which we shall examine here. This book is devoted to a description of the place of music in their lives, to their musical styles, instruments, and history, and to the relationship of primitive music to the music of Western culture.

The study of primitive music falls within the scope of comparative musicology, or, as it is often termed, ethnomusicology, the science that deals with the music of peoples outside of Western civilization. The ethnomusicologist ordinarily distinguishes in his work between three kinds of music: Oriental, folk, and primitive. Oriental music is that of the high cultures of Asia, from China, Japan, and Indonesia to India, Persia, and the Arabic countries. It is not elementary but is cultivated by professional musicians and is in many ways, although not stylistically, comparable to Western European music. Folk music, on the other hand, is the music of social groups which are part of higher cultures but are not themselves musically literate. It is common knowledge that folk songs are often composed anonymously and passed from singer to singer by oral tradition. In this way folk music resembles primitive; the main difference is that the former is always found in a culture that also has cultivated music, which usually influences its style, while the latter belongs to simple cultures that have no writing and are not directly associated with any high cultures.

Of what value is the study of primitive music? There are a number of reasons why ethnomusicologists investigate it. First, it is a new, rich source of experience for Western musicians. With varying degrees of success, many European and American composers have directly or indirectly used material from primitive repertories as bases for compositions — for example, Charles Griffes' phantasy on a Chippewa love song, "First Indian Sketch," and Miecsyslav Kolinski's "Dahomean Suite." Carlos Chávez and Antonín Dvořák, to mention only two among many, have been indirectly influenced by primitive melodies, and some composers have used them almost in their original form. Furthermore, the study and presentation of primitive music widens and enriches the experience of the listener as well as the composer. Many members of Western civilization enjoy listening to primitive music in its original state, as the large number of commercial recordings issued in the past decade adequately testifies.[1] Used as an educational medium, primitive music tends to make a student more tolerant of diverse styles and idioms. If he is learning about certain primitive cultures, contact with their music will make them more alive and real for him; and this method of study is as valid in the elementary schools as in the colleges.

To the historian of music and of culture in general, to the musicologist, anthropologist, folklorist, and psychologist, the study of primitive music is of the greatest importance. The music historian may use it in his efforts to determine the origin of music. Although there is little to be said for the theory that primitive music as we know it now must necessarily be like the music of the Paleolithic cave men, it nevertheless stands to reason that only those traits found in many musical styles, including primitive ones, may safely be considered very old. The study of primitive styles that have been isolated from each other and from cultivated styles for centuries may eventually give at least a comparative basis for a theory of the origin of music. A knowledge of primitive musical styles is also helpful to the psychologist of music. If he is trying to establish universal types of human behavior in respect to music, or if he is trying to formulate the psychological laws by which people react to it, he must take into consideration the many primitive styles and not base his conclusions on Western music alone. The anthropologist and the historian of culture may find through examination of primitive music a substantiation of their theories; the folklorist may see its relationship to the music of rural European populations and be able to trace the latter to its origins; the historian of musical instruments often finds prototypes of European forms in some of the simpler ones in primitive cultures. And the linguist uncovers ethno-linguistic materials. In summary, then, to all people interested in music and to all interested in primitive culture, the study of this music offers new fields for exploration and a wider range for reflection.

We have tentatively defined primitive music by the particular groups of people to whom it belongs rather than by any consideration of its style. This is a necessary distinction, for the styles of the many bodies of primitive music differ from each other as much as they all differ from Oriental, folk, and Western cultivated music. Furthermore, it should be pointed out here that the word "primitive" is not an accurate term for designating the music discussed in this book. We use it because it has been used in the past and is generally accepted by persons acquainted with the material, but it is not actually descriptive. We have no basis for believing that the music labeled "primitive" is closely related to the remote beginnings of the music of the human race: certainly complex styles like those of the African Negroes and the Pueblo Indians of the southwestern United States must have evolved over a long period of time. And assuredly there are many primitive styles that in complexity exceed European and American folk music; in this respect they equal the music of the Oriental high cultures and the European Middle Ages and Renaissance. Therefore we cannot honestly say that the musical styles of the undeveloped cultures are primitive in the sense of being new; so we simply define as primitive that music which is the property of preliterate societies. The burden of designating these societies falls on the shoulders of the anthropologist.

While people are aware generally of the existence of change in Western and Oriental cultures, there is a prevailing attitude, expressed or implied, that primitive cultures are static and have not changed for centuries. The notion is, of course, erroneous. To be sure, many of the primitive traits considered here are still in existence; if such were not the case, recordings of primitive music and information about it would be exceedingly difficult to acquire today. Nevertheless, throughout this book the use of the present tense in statements about the nature and distribution of musical styles does not necessarily indicate the immediate present. I have used an "anthropological" present tense, which is, although technically inaccurate, convenient: it indicates, in the case of each culture for which it is used, the *approximate* time of the group's first contact with Western civilization. The exact date is often difficult to ascertain. Hence the present tense here refers to that period of time, often about a century in length, during which white people gathered information about a primitive group without appreciably changing its culture. This period naturally occurred at different times in different places. The Indians in the eastern part of North America first associated with white men to a significant degree during the seventeenth century; while on the west coast of North America such contact did not take place until the nineteenth. But in our reconstructions of primitive cultures and descriptions of their musical styles, the present tense always refers to the time of first white contact.

The tribal and cultural locations given here are also those of that period. For example, when we speak of the Shawnee Indians of the eastern United States, we mean that they lived in that area of the country around the year 1600, realizing of course that today they live in Oklahoma.

Until fairly recent times, primitive peoples occupied the major portion of the habitable surface of the earth. In Europe today there are no cultures that can be designated as primitive, with the exception of certain parts of European Russia; nor are there any in the Near East and North Africa. In the latter, preliterate peoples with musical styles that might be considered primitive do exist. In view of their close relationship to Islamic culture, however, it is better to call most of their music Arabic folk music, for it bears the same relationship to Arabic cultivated music as European folk songs do to Western cultivated music. South of the Sahara, the continent is inhabited almost entirely by primitive peoples: Negroid, Bushman, Hottentot, Pygmy, Nubian, and Nilotic racial types. There are primitive cultures in Indonesia, Micronesia, Melanesia, the Philippines, Polynesia, Australia, and Siberia, and in various parts of India, southeast Asia, and Malaya. The entire Western hemisphere until approximately 300 years ago was inhabited by American Indians whose cultures were preliterate, with the probable exception of the Mayas of the Yucatan Peninsula, who possessed a form of writing that has not yet been accurately deciphered. Despite their widespread territorial distribution, however, primitive tribes have generally consisted of relatively few members. The Indians of both North and South America are estimated to have numbered only nine million, and Australia and Polynesia have few inhabitants. Somewhat denser primitive populations are found in Africa, India, and Indonesia.

Primitive cultures and musical styles in these various areas differ considerably, and we are far from knowing them comprehensively. A few musical styles are known intimately and documented accurately; some are known only slightly; while others again are vitually unknown. Even so, the amount of material available is so great and the variety so striking that in this book we shall have to be content with describing thoroughly only one or two large areas and pointing out more briefly some isolated examples.

2

The role of music in primitive culture

THE FUNCTIONS OF PRIMITIVE MUSIC

Music is a phenomenon present in all cultures, primitive and civilized. This very fact indicates how ancient it must be; only a few other cultural traits share its world-wide distribution. In primitive societies, music frequently plays a far more important role than in Western civilization.[1] The stylistically simple music of a primitive tribe often has great prominence within its culture because of its prevailing functionality: most primitive music (despite some notable exceptions) serves a particular purpose other than providing pure entertainment or aesthetic enjoyment. This does not mean that a great deal of music does not also serve as entertainment or that its producers and listeners do not enjoy it. But, if questioned, native informants almost always indicate some exterior purpose for their music.

Probably its most important and most frequent use is assisting in religious rituals. Every tribe uses music somehow in its ceremonies, although the forms vary considerably. For example, among the Yuman tribes of Arizona and Southern California, songs are interspersed throughout tribal myths which carry religious significance.[2] These myths are in a way analogous to our Bible. They are recited aloud — a process that may take several days — and periodically during the recitation the raconteur sings songs that are related to the story. In a great many primitive religious rites, dancing plays an important part. It is almost always accompanied by music; hence many primitive dance songs are basically religious in function.

Occasionally religious ceremonies consist almost entirely of songs, as is the case in the Peyote cult of many North American Indian tribes.[3] That cult, adopted by Indians in the United States from Mexican tribes within the last three centuries, holds all-night meetings at which the members chew the slightly intoxicating buttons of the Peyote cactus and sing songs in a style different from that of their other music. The Peyote songs often have meaningless texts, and, where the texts are meaningful, they rarely deal with the Peyote plant or other aspects of the ceremony.

Music sometimes establishes connections between religious and other activities. Again the North American Indians come to mind; some of them use music as a part of gambling and hiding games.[4] Two teams alternate in hiding from each other a small object. While one team searches for it, the hiding team often sing songs that have two purposes: to invoke supernatural aid in preventing their opponents from finding the object, and to help the singers keep a straight face and not give the secret away by facial expression or laughter. Here music is the link with the supernatural in a playful activity not directly associated with religion. It is this sort of situation, found throughout the world, which prompted Siegfried Nadel to form the theory that music came into existence from the desire of primitive peoples to have a special language other than ordinary speech for communication with the supernatural.[5] This theory, although unprovable, originated from the massive amount of evidence that there is a special and close connection between music and religion in most primitive cultures.

Perhaps the next most prevalent use of music is as an accompaniment to nonreligious dances. In most primitive cultures, songs and instrumental music are frequently associated with social dancing; some of the song texts are simple lyrical love songs in the Western sense of the word, and others are love charms having religious or magical connotations.

Love songs in many parts of the world are associated with flutes. Because primitive love songs are frequently designed to be either sung or played on the flute, and because the use of the flute is often restricted to love charms, the theory has evolved that this instrument is primarily a symbol of the male sex organ. According to Curt Sachs, among others, most instruments have some kind of sexual symbolism, which may be manifested either in the structure of the instrument or in its assocation with the sex of the player.[6] This topic is considered later in the discussion of musical instruments in Chapter 7, but its significance for the function of music in primitive culture is obvious.

Music also frequently plays an important part in story-telling. Throughout the world, songs are inserted into stories, as much in Western European folk cultures as in primitive ones. In Grimm's tale of the man who caught the king of fishes, the fish is called from the water with this song:

> O man of the sea!
> Come listen to me,
> For Alice my wife,
> The plague of my life,
> Hath sent me to beg a boon of thee![7]

The music is not printed in the Grimm collection, but the song is often sung rather than recited by folk tellers. Similar cases are found among primitive people. In Negro Africa especially, songs are important in tales. The Lamba of Northern Rhodesia have two kinds of tales, ordinary and choric,[8] and a great amount of singing takes place in the choric tales. A given song recurs at various points in the story, and the audience sings it with the raconteur. Since the usual style of these songs is responsorial in some sense, the teller has the musical role of leader and the audience of chorus. Example 1, from the Shona Karanga in South Africa, is a song from a choric tale. The texts of such songs rarely, if ever, further the plot; they are lyrical and often related to supernatural elements in the tales, as in the story of the king of fishes.

Primitive people hardly ever use music as the sole vehicle for relating a long story. However, a few rare cases of narrative songs have been discovered. One found among the Paiute Indians of

Nevada has been described by Edward Sapir.[9] A similar phenomenon is found among the Northern Utes and discussed by Frances Densmore. They sing short animal tales, with new melodic material provided for each section of the text.[10] In this case the entire tale is sung, and the style of these songs is simpler than that of others in the same area. Short narrative songs are also sung by the Plains Indians. The men sometimes sing them at gatherings after war parties; the texts deal with their martial exploits — for example, "The Ute Indian, while he was looking around for me, I scalped him alive." [11] Often one melody has its text changed periodically to conform to events of current interest. After World War I, when some American Indians returned from the European battlefields, this song text was made up for the occasion: "Germany wants to fight, but is no good at all." [12] Longer narratives, corresponding to the ballads of European folk tradition, are practically never found in any primitive group.

This leads us naturally to another tribal experience in which music is functional: war. Although war songs are connected with religion in many cultures (they may solicit supernatural aid to assure success in battle) and are once in a while of a narrative nature, they occasionally take a special form among primitive peoples similar to our cheers in athletics. Among the Ibo of Nigeria, the following incantation is used to rally the warriors before an attack: "The Ibo people are like the elephant." [13]

Music as a means of entertainment occurs only in areas where both culture and musical style are relatively complex. One such place is Negro Africa, where some of the royal potentates, such as the kings of Ashanti and Dahomey, have professional musicians who play only for the king's pleasure. In French Equatorial Africa, xylophone players are engaged to provide music on market days for the amusement of the crowd. The use of music in songs of praise, also found in Africa, falls likewise into this category.[14]

Instrumental signaling relates music to language in a rather specialized way. It is sometimes connected directly with the language and sometimes consists of a simple code. In the former case, the language is almost always a tone language, that is, one in which the pitch differences of the individual syllables carry lexical differentiation. An instrumental tone is substituted for a speech tone, and the speech-melody pattern of the language is thus reproduced in the signaling. The use of tones in a language is a musical phenomenon in itself, but the subject of tone languages and signaling is too complex to be elaborated here; the best we can do is to cite works by Kenneth L. Pike and George Herzog as suggested reading.[15] However, musical signaling must certainly be included as one of the functions of music in primitive cultures: drum signaling is found throughout Negro Africa, in Melanesia, and among Middle American Indian tribes; horn signaling is found in Central and West Africa; and signal-whistling among some Mexican tribes.

It is difficult to find any *essential* difference between the role of music in primitive societies and the role of music in high cultures, for, although functional music predominates in primitive cultures, it is also found to a considerable extent in Western cultivated societies. The chief distinction in role is quantitative: among primitive people, functional music is far more frequent in proportion to the total amount of music performed.

MUSICAL SPECIALIZATION WITHIN PRIMITIVE GROUPS

One aspect which may be unique to primitive cultures is the general participation of all members of a tribe in music. Such general participation occurs to some extent in most of their activities. The typical primitive group has no specialization or professionalization; its division of labor depends almost exclusively on sex and occasionally on age; and only rarely are certain individuals proficient in any technique to a distinctive degree. All women do the same things each day, possess approximately the same skills, have the same interests; and the men's activities are equally common to all. Accordingly, the same songs are known by all the members of the group, and there is little specialization in composition, performance, or instrument-making.

There are, however, many modifications and exceptions to this generalization. First, there is in music the usual differentiation according to sex. In most North American Indian tribes, for example, men are more important in musical activities. They lead the singing; they do most of the composing; and they do a greater amount of performing than women. Conversely, in some African Negro tribes women usually lead the songs, because of their strong voices, ability to compose, and more extensive knowledge of the material. This is also true in certain Negro cultures of the New World, notably in the West Indies.[16] Frequently there is also a sort of specialization not recognized by the culture in an official sense but based on individual differences in musical ability. In most cultures a few people are acknowledged to be the best singers. The criteria used to determine "the best" are not often known, but they are believed to vary considerably: sometimes the people with the loudest voices are considered the best; elsewhere the honor goes to the ones knowing the most songs.

Specialization in composition will be discussed later in more detail. It should be noted here that proficiency in composition occasionally correlates with maladjustment to the culture and is often associated with religious activity.[17] Among many American Indian and some Paleo-Siberian tribes, composition is ordinarily relegated to shamans (medicine-men) or other individuals connected with religion in a particular way. Indeed, musical and religious specialization are often correlated, and are probably the two activities of primitive life in which specialization most commonly occurs.

There are some primitive cultures, however, where professional musicians in the true sense of the word are found. They are generally present only in the relatively advanced cultures that have nonfunctional music and a complex style, particularly in instrumental music. Such cultures exist in some parts of Negro Africa. We have mentioned previously the royal orchestras and the xylophone players at markets. Players of signal drums and horns in Africa also have semiprofessional status.

There is one marked exception to the statement that primitive people rarely differentiate between composers and performers. Hugh Tracey tells us that the Chopi of Portuguese East Africa possess semiprofessional xylophone orchestras, led by conductors

who are also composers and poets.[18] However, it is probable that
the entire Chopi system of xylophone orchestras, elaborate techniques of composition, and the common use of heterophony is an
importation from Indonesia via Madagascar.[19] Since most evidence points to the fact that the xylophone itself was imported
into Africa from the Indonesian high cultures around A.D. 500,
near the area that the Chopi inhabit today, this assumption is
credible.

On the whole, then, we can find little differentiation in primitive cultures between composer, performer, and listener. The role
of composition is frequently misunderstood by Western observers,
partly because of this situation and partly because of the common
fallacy that primitive cultures consist entirely of undifferentiated
masses.

TECHNIQUES OF COMPOSITION

In this section we will discuss and illustrate several kinds of
musical composition found among preliterate peoples. No generalizations can be made contrasting the techniques of composition of primitive music with those of cultivated music, except
the obvious one that the latter is written down. The range of
primitive methods extends from various subconscious and im-
provisatory processes to skilled ones comparable to those used by
Western composers. Folklore and anthropological theory have
established one point of general agreement about primitive
composition: any item of music — a song, an instrumental piece,
or a song series — is produced by one individual or by a group
of individuals, who work with material which they have acquired
through experience. Primitive music is very similar to cultivated
in that its creation can be traced to one or more persons, for most
people by now have rejected the idea that even folk music is
created communally, that it evolved from the collective imagina-
tion of the masses.

It was believed at one time that the main primitive method of
composition was improvisation during the performance of music.
This actually occurs in only a minority of cases. To be sure, a
native composer does improvise by himself, perhaps in an isolated

spot, but he does not consider that the same thing as a public performance. He works on his composition alone, going over it, changing parts, adding and subtracting material. He has to accomplish the task by singing or playing because he has no way to write down his composition; a Western composer does the same thing when he makes changes, additions, and deletions with his pen. When real improvisation in public does take place, it is usually associated with a special function and the improviser recognized as a person of unusual skill.

However, some tribes do practice on-the-spot improvisation. One of the most interesting cases is that of the Greenland Eskimos, who sing songs with a legal function.[20] No forms of physical combat or war are customarily present in Eskimo culture; they are not sanctioned nor is their existence recognized by the tribes. If two men have a disagreement and begin physical fighting, an older man intervenes and stops them, at the same time making an appointment for the fighters to have what the natives call a "drum dance." The entire community attends this meeting, and the two adversaries take turns in singing derisive songs at each other, accompanied by mocking gestures. The man whose songs best drive home his point, according to the consensus of public opinion, wins the fight. There are rarely any further antagonistic incidents. These juridical songs, which deal with actual situations and events in the lives of the individuals concerned, are supposed to be improvised. It is quite possible that the contestants do prepare their songs ahead of time, at least partially, but such preparation is not recognized by the culture.

This improvisation by the Eskimos is presumably done without the use of any extant compositions or melodic formulas. A much more widespread phenomenon is changing or improvising on a melody already known, which is sometimes called "communal re-creation" and is certainly present to some extent in all traditional music. In other words, we assume that every singer changes a song slightly from the version he has learned. Indeed, Phillips Barry, a pioneer scholar in American folk music, considered communal re-creation the essential factor in folk music.[21] Barry's theory at present stands in need of some revision, in the light of recent discoveries; for example, he held that forgetfulness and the momentary whims of individual singers are responsible for most changes in folk songs, while it appears now that multiple versions have been caused by general aesthetic and cultural conditions. Nonetheless, it is likely that communal re-creation occurs not only in folk songs but in the music of all preliterate people, whether they realize it or not.

The amount of primitive re-creation permitted by the tribe varies a great deal. It is ostentatiously encouraged in some cultures but frowned on or forbidden in others. Among some North American Indians it is prevented by fear of error as well as by technical means. The Navaho Indians have long series of songs associated with curing rituals,[22] and they take special care to ascertain that each song is performed correctly and in the right order. Mistakes are serious enough to invalidate the entire ceremony. We do not know yet how much deviation is considered a mistake — whether it is the singing of a note out of tune, or the omission of an entire phrase — but we do know that errors, however defined, are not allowed. The Indians of the Northwest Pacific Coast, whose musical style is one of the most complex on the continent, go even further. In order to assure a minimum number of errors, songs are systematically rehearsed and mistakes in performance are punished.[23]

On the other hand, such improvisation is encouraged among many African Negro tribes. It is intimately connected with the antiphonal and responsorial techniques characteristic of much of their music. In many of their compositions, phrases or sections occur in pairs, to be sung or played once by a leader and once by a chorus. One part (usually the chorus) tends to repeat its melody without changes, while the other part tends to vary and develop its part with each repetition. The basic melody of the song exists before the performance; the variations are improvised during it. Out of that one melody come many related variants, through the process of communal re-creation. Example 2 illustrates such an antiphonal song.

In most tribes there are certain recognized ways in which individuals can acquire songs. The ways are sometimes realistic and indicative of actual conditions, but more often they are designed to hide the real processes in order to associate them with the supernatural in the mind of the noncomposer. One important method is learning from other individuals, either in the same tribe or from the outside. But the other methods of acquiring songs are the relevant ones for the study of musical composition. Among the North American Indians there are two important ways in which new songs can be acquired: conscious composition, a process akin to that of Western composers; and learning songs in visions or dreams. The latter is of considerable interest because of its wide distribution; it is found in most tribes west of the Mississippi River.

Among the Indians of the Great Plains of Montana, Colorado, and Wyoming, the acquisition of songs in visions carries prestige value and is part of the experience of most men. The vision quest of the Plains Indians is typically associated with asceticism. A man goes out into the wilderness by himself, fasts, and tortures himself by cutting his flesh or even cutting off a finger, until he receives a vision. It is usually in the form of an animal, which gives him advice and often teaches him one or more songs. Some of the songs are intended to be part of a ceremony; some have no special function; and occasionally the vision songs are not to be sung until a time of particular stress arises, such as illness or death. The visionary then returns to his tribe and carries out the instructions of the vision being. Frequently the texts of these songs are concerned with what the vision being was saying when he first appeared; for example, a typical text, from the Arapaho of Wyoming, is "Look up here, I am the bird." [24]

Each man in most of the Plains tribes is supposed to have at least one such vision during his life, and many have several. Thus we may infer that practically all of them are composers, although the acquisition of a "new" song sometimes means merely the creation of a new text for an old melody. If a man does not have a vision in spite of his quest, he will occasionally invent one and consciously compose the requisite songs in order to avoid the loss of prestige which would accompany an unsuccessful attempt. Examples of fabricated visions have been documented.[25] Such deception has been known to lead to feelings of guilt and resulting maladjusted behavior in some individuals, which shows clearly the distinction that these Indians make between vision composition and conscious composition.

The Yuman tribes of Arizona and Southern California recognize only music created in dreams; conscious composition is not admitted at all.[26] Very few of their members are capable of dreaming songs, and some of those so gifted are definitely neurotic in their adjustment to their culture. This condition may be connected with the fact that group singing is exceedingly rare among the Yuman Indians, while solo singing is the rule, in contrast to the Great Plains Indians. It is especially interesting that the Yumans do not recognize the learning of songs already in existence. If an individual wishes to sing a song dreamt by another he must dream it again himself; the only way songs can be learned, whether they are old or new, is through dreams.

It is difficult to do research on the techniques of conscious composition of the North American Indians, because the natives do not ordinarily discuss such matters among themselves. Consequently native informants have trouble explaining the techniques to investigators, and the confusion is heightened by the fact that most investigators are unfortunately not trained musicologically. Yet we do have information on the subject that merits examination, and shall consider here a few outstanding examples of conscious composition.

The methods used by the Peyote cult of the Great Plains are well suited to our purpose, for the tradition is alive and productively operating today. The Peyote cult was diffused among the Great Plains Indians within the last one hundred and fifty years by tribes in northern Mexico and the southwestern United States. It is superficially connected with Christianity and is incorporated, like a church, with an intertribal organization.[27] The musical style of the Peyote songs differs from that of the other songs of the Plains Indians; it is characterized by the use of two note values in each song, by relatively quick tempo, relaxed vocal technique, and a closing formula on the tonic that consists of four even notes. These properties recur in an overwhelming proportion of Peyote songs and are rare in the others of the Plains. While the other songs, those used for war, social dancing, love, etc., are being composed only sparsely today, and the repertory consists primarily of traditional material, Peyote songs are being created in profusion. One tribe teaches them to another, and individual songs often have a wide distribution.

An Arapaho Indian who was able to verbalize to some extent about composition [28] gave me the following information about two Peyote methods. Both involve the use of previously existing material, and, although they are probably not the only methods practiced, they do account for a considerable number of songs.

When listening to Peyote songs, one is alerted by the astonishing homogeneity of style; indeed, one hears the same melodies repeated over and over. The informant's explanation of this was that one method of composition is to borrow material freely from extant songs. The composer takes a phrase from one song, another from a second, inserts perhaps one or two original phrases, and appends the traditional closing formula. Examples 3 and 4 are songs composed in this way; they begin almost identically and diverge later. (Example 4 has an introduction; the main body of the song begins after the first double bar.) The devotees of the cult, rather surprisingly, often remember who composed a particular song and sometimes identify it by the composer's name.

The second technique described by my informant is to shorten, lengthen, or make substitutions in a song so extensively that the end result is a new song. Evidently not much alteration is required to change the identity of a song in the mind of the Arapaho. This method of composition is illustrated by Example 5, which presents two Shawnee Peyote songs. The first, like many Peyote songs, consists of isorhythmic or modified isorhythmic phrases: that is, a rhythmic formula is repeated many times, each time with a different melody. The second song was apparently composed with the first as a basis. The only change made was to add a note at the end of each isorhythmic unit. The song texts (which are not reproduced here) are both meaningless, so we know that the change was not caused by any textual demands. My informant considered these songs as separate but admitted that they are similar. Because of the frequency of isorhythmic material in Peyote songs, this method of composition seems to be important.

These techniques of conscious composition both involve re-working old material into new songs. Unfortunately, at present we do not know enough about the creation of entirely original songs by the Plains Indians to discuss it profitably. The current theory is that the bulk of their music is a revision of older material, and that this accounts for the great homogeneity of some Indian styles.

The musical styles of the African Negroes are generally more complex than those of the North American Indians, and the composition techniques of at least some African cultures are accordingly more sophisticated. Certain African tribes that speak in tone languages use phrases or words as the basis for musical motifs; their patterns of speech melody serve as the foundation for musical compositions. For example, xylophone players in Liberia employ the tone sequence of one word in making a short motif on which is based a more complex composition.[29] Sometimes they combine two such motifs to form a short piece of free poloyphony.

In *Chopi Musicians*, Hugh Tracey describes what is believed to be the most sophisticated method of composition yet found among preliterate peoples. The Chopi, as we have mentioned already, have made great progress in xylophone-building, albeit they probably derived the skill from another culture (see the discussion on page 98). Their xylophones are made in four sizes, and an orchestra is composed of about ten instruments. It is used to accompany long ceremonial and spectacular dances. The leader of the orchestra combines with the functions of conductor and performer those of composer and poet; he creates both music and text of a long composition known as the *ngomi*. A *ngomi* begins with an orchestral overture and consists of about ten dance movements in different tempos and styles. The composer first produces the text, which is usually lyrical and concerned with situations in the contemporary affairs of the Chopi; then he starts to work on the music. Since Chopi is a tone language, he often uses the tones of the text as the basis for the first musical theme. He develops the theme by improvisation, and his apparently excellent memory enables him to reproduce quite accurately in performance the improvisations he has evolved in private. Next he composes a second theme that is contrapuntal in relation to the first. The other xylophone players partially improvise their parts in accordance with the styles of their various instruments, and they also follow the verbal instructions of the leader. The entire composition is rehearsed. The final preparatory step is a consultation between the leader and the chief choreographer, who also has rather sophisticated techniques at his command. Together these masters change, rework, and assimilate their creation. The joint public performance of dance and music is concertlike in nature. In this culture, then, we have an unusual example of conscious composition as well as of specialization of activities, and, fortunately, the native composers seem to have little difficulty in verbalizing about the process.

Preliterate peoples in general have one of two prevalent attitudes towards composition. Some of them consider it a craft, consciously practiced by the composer; others associate it with the supernatural and believe the composer to be a tool of mysterious powers over which he has no control. Both attitudes are, of course, also found among members of Western culture.

We have seen from the foregoing samples of primitive composition techniques how greatly they vary from culture to culture. We have examined sophisticated methods of conscious composition, types of unconscious composition that resemble our concept of inspiration, and other methods based on improvisation. We have demonstrated that each culture recognizes certain ways of acquiring musical material and that some of the ways are more realistic than others. It is to be hoped that further research on composition will eventually lead to a better understanding of the genesis of primitive musical styles and of the psychological processes of composition common to all cultures.

THE PROCESS OF EVALUATION

An attempt to evaluate primitive music according to Western standards is futile, for unless the Western auditor is well acquainted with this form of music such an attempt will merely reveal his prejudices.[30] He will naturally prefer the musical styles that are close to his own and stress features important in Western music, such as harmony and polyphony. It would be definitely valuable, however, to do further research on the evaluation of music within the preliterate cultures themselves. This area has been neglected by field investigators; the only specialized study of it was done by Herzog, who has published some brief statements about music in the thinking of certain American Indian tribes (see the bibliography).

The concept of music as "beautiful" seems to be generally undeveloped in primitive cultures. Informants speak of songs as being "good." No doubt the prevailing functionality of music is responsible for this designation, for beauty is an end in itself, while "good" implies usefulness for a specific purpose: a song may be good for curing, good for dancing, etc. In some tribes informants also describe songs as "powerful," probably because the songs have some sort of supernatural function. J. S. Slotkin his published a record of his conversations with a Menomini Indian on this subject.[31]

As we have already seen, the identification of a "good" singer varies from tribe to tribe. Among the Arapaho Indians of Wyoming, for example, a good singer is one who knows a great many songs. With other tribes, voice quality is the determining factor. On the Great Plains of North America a singer with a high voice is considered admirable; in the Pueblos of Arizona and New Mexico a low, growling voice is preferred; and the discrepancy is all the more interesting because the musical styles found in these two areas are related.

The degree of preference for music of tribes other than one's own also varies. The Ibo of Nigeria prefer their own old songs, uninfluenced by the music of any other tribe. The Plains Indians, on the other hand, are usually glad to learn songs from the outside and to admit the fact. The vast majority of primitive peoples have probably learned a great deal of their music from others, and such transfer can be observed in operation today under relatively aboriginal conditions in some parts of the world. But attitudes towards such borrowing are quite dissimilar. When the Plains Indians are asked about the sources of their songs, they not only cheerfully acknowledge the origin but even remember the tribe from which the material stems. The Pima of Arizona have quite the opposite attitude: some of their songs that have obviously been borrowed from the neighboring Yuman tribes and are sung in the Yuman language are explained by the Pima themselves as being "old Pima songs." [32] These examples emphasize not only variation in attitudes towards borrowing music but also the great variety of conditions throughout primitive musical styles and the consequent difficulty of making any valid generalizations.

THE RELATIONSHIP OF MUSIC AND LANGUAGE

The relationship of music and language has been touched on already in our discussions of instrumental signaling and the Chopi xylophone orchestras, both of which use the speech patterns of tone languages as a basis for musical composition. We shall now consider in more detail some special aspects of this relationship in primitive cultures.

Song texts and melodies. Most primitive people seem to conceive of the words and melody of a song as one unit that cannot be separated. Native informants are rarely able to differentiate between them, nor can native singers ordinarily give either text or music alone without difficulty. In spite of this, however, we cannot devise far-reaching theories about the common origin of a tune and its text, for we know that in many cases texts are changed while melodies remain intact, and that in other cases the same text may be sung to several different melodies. As an example of the former, we cite again the practice of the Plains Indians in keeping the texts of their war songs up-to-date.

The textual organization of most primitive music, especially

that of the American Indians, is not like the textual organization
of folk music. It does not usually depend on the line as the basic
unit. Often primitive song texts have neither rhyme nor meter,
nor a syllabic arrangement of any sort. They do have a great deal
of repetition and variation, as the following text illustrates.

> Where the talagoya was roasted and eaten,
>   there blew a wind.
> Where the meminna was roasted and eaten,
>   there blew a wind.
> Where the deer was roasted and eaten,
>   there blew a wind.[33]

When tribes such as the Plains Indians replace one song text
by another of different length, the problem arises of how to fit
the new words to the melody. The Plains Indians usually solve it
very nicely by making their melodies longer than their texts in
the first place, and then filling in with meaningless syllables
any left-over melodic parts. Many of their songs consist of two
large sections, the second a variation of the first. Meaningless
syllables comprise the first section; the text begins with the second but is not long enough to cover the entire melody, so that
the song ends with meaningless syllables again.

Meaningless syllables. In a great many primitive styles, such
meaningless syllables are used as partial or complete song texts.
This is particularly true among the North American Indians,
who have quantities of songs with texts composed entirely of
them. Practically all songs in some tribes contain at least a few.
The structure of these syllables is illuminating. Let us turn to
the Peyote cult once again for an example of particular interest.
Approximately one-half of the Peyote songs have nonsense texts,
although the proportion varies from tribe to tribe: most of the
Comanche Peyote songs have meaningful texts,[34] whereas most
of the Arapaho do not.

The meaningless syllables of Peyote songs are distinguished
from those of other songs in the same tribal repertories by the
use of additional consonants and by their peculiar organization
into wordlike patterns or sequences. Both the Peyote and the

non-Peyote songs of the Arapaho and the Shawnee tribes make much use of the consonants *y, w,* and *h.* But *c, k, t, x,*[35] and *n* are found frequently in the Peyote songs and rarely, if ever, in the others. A meaningless Peyote syllable usually contains one of these consonants and one vowel. The syllables are grouped into sequences that resemble words, and these sequences recur in songs of tribes having diverse unrelated languages. McAllester cites *he yo wi ci ha yo* as the most characteristic.[36] Typical Arapaho syllabic sequences are *yo wi ci ni, he yo wi ci, wi ci hay, yo wa ni,* and *ye no wi ci.* Here is an Arapaho meaningless Peyote text in its entirety:

> *ye no wi ci hay*
> *yo wi hay*
> *wi ci hay*
> *yo wi ci no*
> *wi ci ni*
>
> (Repeat from start)
>
> *wi ni wi ci hay*
> *yo wi hay*
> *wi ci hay*
> *yo wi ci ni hay*
> *yo wi ci ni hay*
> *yo wi how*
> *wi ci hay*
> *yo wi ci no*
> *wi hi no wa* [37]

The relationship of the meaningless sequences to the musical structure is interesting in the following ways. Many songs have an isorhythmic structure — a single rhythmic pattern is repeated throughout. Deviations from the pattern usually occur at the end of the song and sometimes at the end of major subdivisions. Other songs, while not entirely isorhythmic, contain isorhythmic sections: a rhythmic pattern is repeated several times but does not dominate the entire structure. Still others use a number (often three or four) of rhythmic patterns, which are alternated or repeated; each is likely to recur several times.

In many of the songs, the sequences of meaningless syllables are correlated with the rhythmic construction. An isorhythmic song is likely to employ the same syllabic sequence for each repetition of the rhythmic unit. If several rhythmic units are used in the song, the syllabic sequence differs for each, and the same sequence usually accompanies each recurrence of one pattern.

The closing formula of Peyote songs consists of four long notes or of three long notes and one short one; it is sung on the tonic, and the accompanying syllables are frequently *he ne yo wa.* The device of a closing formula composed of the repeated tonic or final tone is not limited to Peyote songs, but this form, with some variations, is characteristic of them. The closing syllables are modified according to rather rigid rules. Consonants other than those in *he ne yo wa* are permitted. The vowels may be changed, but their mutual relationship in regard to their articulatory position must remain constant: the vowels of the first and second syllables are always the same and are usually either higher than or identical with the vowel of the fourth syllable. The following Arapaho and Shawnee closing formulas fit these prescriptions: *he ne yo we, he te no we, ni wi no wi, hi wi yo we, hi ti no wa, ni wi yo we.*[38]

Although it is possible that the Peyote syllabic sequences were derived from meaningful words in the language of one of the tribes from which the cult originally spread, no evidence for such an assumption has come to light yet. The complexity of these meaningless texts appears to be rather uncommon in North American Indian songs, and their relationship to the rhythmic structure of the songs is fascinating.

Correlating analogous features. A universal problem in the relationship between language and music is that of correlating certain analogous features in these two forms of communication. Pitch, stress, and length are found in both music and language and are significant in many languages. The student of this problem tries to discover whether syllables spoken on a high pitch by a certain linguistic group are also sung high when they occur in a song text, whether vowels stressed or sustained in speech are also sung that way, etc. Such studies may eventually indicate whether linguistic patterns have a great deal of influence on the musical styles of various peoples, or whether linguistic features are violated when musical laws are superimposed on sung texts. Needless to say, this problem merits study not only in primitive music but also in folk, Oriental, and Western cultivated styles.

No generalizations can be made about the influence of language on primitive musical styles. The facts as usual vary from tribe to tribe. Language seems to have influenced musical styles to some extent, but it certainly has not dominated their development. In many cases, linguistic features are violated when words are combined with music. It is impossible now to say that in any particular culture the music is definitely subordinate to the language or vice versa.[39]

Primitive tone symbolism. The most obscure and complicated aspect of the relationship between music and language is symbolism, or tone-painting. Although this concept poses difficult problems in Western music, it is even harder to pin down in primitive. Native informants are able to say almost nothing on the symbolic aspect of their music, and we do not know the styles intimately enough to draw conclusions through direct musical evidence alone. Probably symbolism is present in a few styles, at least, and the investigator should always be aware of that possibility. But so far nothing definitive has been discovered. Only a few examples of imitation of animal calls have been found in primitive music. In some cases the singer imitates the animal call as naturalistically as possible before, during, or after the song, which cannot be considered true tone-painting in any sense of the word. But in other cases the animal cry is not imitated with an attempt at strict realism; the cry is part of the song, fitting into the musical style in scale, ryhthm, and form. Because of its stylistic conformity, this can be considered true musical symbolism. Example 6 is a Shawnee song of this type, in which the call of the wild female turkey is imitated at the end. On being questioned, the Shawnee informants admitted that they recognized the representation for what it was.

3

The development and disciplines of ethnomusicology

Although the scientific and scholarly study of primitive music originated relatively recently, European musicians have been concerned with the music of non-European peoples for several centuries. As early as the Renaissance, we find Orlando di Lasso evidently interested in the music of Neapolitan Negroes and writing compositions based to some extent on their style.[1] About the same time, Spanish missionaries in Mexico were in contact with Mexican Indian music, and possibly some of their compositions were influenced by it, although the evidence is slim because of the dearth of information on Mexican Indian music, especially of the Mexican high cultures.[2] It was during the Renaissance, the time in which the Western world discovered that the ancient Greeks had had a rich musical culture and had left an extensive literature on their musical aesthetic, that musicians first became conscious of the wealth of material outside of their own culture. This realization was confined, however, to relatively few individuals, and certainly nothing of a scientific nature was connected with it.

Not until the late eighteenth century did scholars actually become aware of the importance of non-Western material for students of music. One of the early landmarks is the *Dictionary of Music* of Jean Jacques Rousseau, which appeared in 1768 and foreshadows the development of the three branches of comparative musicology. The appendix to Rousseau's dictionary includes one transcription for each branch: a Chinese melody for Oriental cultivated music, a Canadian Indian song for primitive, and a Swiss folk song. Today it is taken for granted that an ethnomusicologist should know something of all three fields, which are related only by virtue of their contrast with Western cultivated music. Of the three, primitive music is the latest to be thoroughly explored.

It was during Rousseau's day that the serious study of Oriental music was begun. The early books on Chinese music by Père Joseph Amiot, Indian music by William Jones, and Arabic music by Raphael G. Kiesewetter are significant.[3] Meanwhile, spurred on by the romantic movement, folk music also became prominent. Philosophers and literary artists like Herder, the Grimm brothers, and Goethe were mainly concerned with the texts of folk songs, but their interest also encompassed the music. In the early nineteenth century we find, of course, the beginning of national styles among composers, styles that were to some extent based on or influenced by regional folk music. The fact that folk music was unearthed during the romantic movement naturally led to theories about its origin that reflect the idealistic romantic viewpoint towards folklore. In this period the theory of the communal origin of folk music was first propounded, according to which music, in some mystical way, emanated from "the people." Although there is more than a grain of truth to this idea, as we have seen in the discussion of primitive composition, on the whole it is certainly not compatible with modern anthropological theory. Still, it is accepted by a surprisingly large number of individuals even today.

Least closely related to Western cultivated music in both style and cultural position, and last to come to the attention of the musicologist, was primitive music. One landmark for the beginning of scholarly study is a short monograph by the German philosopher and psychologist Carl Stumpf on the music of the Bella Coola Indians of British Columbia.[4] In 1882 a group of Bella Coola Indians visited Berlin, where they performed songs and dances; and Stumpf, intrigued by their songs, worked for many hours with one singer, writing down the songs in modern

musical notation. This experience stimulated him to further
study of primitive and Oriental music, and eventually he founded
the Berlin archives. About the same time, Alexander J. Ellis, a
British physicist and acoustician, also became interested in primitive and Oriental music. Ellis was active primarily in the study
of tone systems and in measuring the intervals of non-European
scales. In his main work [5] he introduced the cent system of
measuring tones, which was subsequently adopted by comparative musicologists as well as by practicing musicians. It is based
on the cent, a unit that is one per cent of a tempered half tone.
An octave has 1,200 cents. For example, the theoretical Arabic
scale of Al-Kindi, from the tenth century, would be analyzed
according to cents in the following way: the lowest, or basic, tone
is 0; the others, in terms of their distance from the basic tone, are
90, 180, 204, 294, 384, 408, 498, 588, 612, 702, 792, 816,
906, 1020, 1110, 1200.[6] This scale consists of tones slightly
smaller than half tones, interspersed with tones about one-eighth
the size of a whole tone. The cent system has been widely used
to indicate the intervals of primitive scales and is easier to
handle than vibration rates that operate in terms of ratios rather
than simple integers.

Stumpf and Ellis, the pioneers of modern ethnomusicology,
were the first of that group of scholars that we shall call for lack
of a better name the German school of comparative musicology.
In contrast to it there was a parallel development in the United
States that we shall call the American school. These two groups
were the most important both in beginning and in propagating
the study; the scholars in other countries were less active and less
concentrated.

The German school was composed largely of psychologists,
and its leaders — Stumpf and later Erich M. von Hornbostel —
were psychologists at the University of Berlin. Their interest in
music was naturally largely influenced by this discipline, and
they realized that, in order to arrive at any understanding of the
place of music in the framework of the human mind, they could
not limit their research to the music of one culture but must
include that of many societies. They were joined by scholars of

acoustics and of the physiological aspects of music, who were interested in the study of intervals, tone measurements, and tone systems. Thus we find the German school primarily concerned with melodic and pitch phenomena, with scales, intervals, and tone systems, with less emphasis on other equally important aspects such as rhythm, form, and vocal technique. They developed theories on the origins of music that largely depended on pitch phenomena. In general, they emphasized the analysis of musical styles as such, rather than their relationship to their cultures.

The latter interest predominated in the American school, for it consisted mainly of anthropologists and practicing musicians. They were not well versed in methods of musicological analysis or in general theories of musical development. They were students of primitive culture, first, and they found music an interesting and important possession of every tribe they studied. Accordingly, their emphasis was on presenting this musical material in its original form and showing its place within its culture. For a time these students could hardly even be considered a school, because they were individual scholars isolated not only from each other but also from the European centers of learning; and, in consequence, their progress was slow. After contact with European comparative musicologists was made, however, the anthropological emphasis of the Americans began to contribute a great deal to the field as a whole.

What is the reason for the divergence in interest of the German and American scholars? Besides their differing original disciplines, it may well be due to geographic location. The Germans were distant from primitive peoples. They examined the musical material in archives in Germany and had relatively little firsthand knowledge of the cultures whose music they were studying. The Americans, on the other hand, were close to a rich field of primitive culture, the American Indians. It was easy for them to make field trips to hear Indian music in its original setting; hence, probably, came the preoccupation of Americans with the cultural integration of music and their relative inattention to scientific analysis of the music itself.

The perfection of the phonograph around 1890 eventually

brought about tremendous changes in the methodology of comparative musicologists. It made possible the transference of music from its native surroundings to laboratories where it could be studied. Stumpf had had to notate his Bella Coola songs from informants who were willing to repeat a song many times, for in order to make the transcription as accurate as possible he had to hear each section over and over. Besides the possibly limited patience of his informants, he had to cope with the fact that each rendition might be slightly different from the others. With the advent of the phonograph, of course, this whole process was outmoded; repetition of the same rendition became a simple matter, with absolute uniformity guaranteed. One could compare separated parts of a song by playing them in succession, and there was no limit on the length of the segments played.

If Stumpf may be considered the grandfather of comparative musicology, his student, assistant, and successor Erich M. von Hornbostel may be called its father. Hornbostel was the first to explore many styles of primitive and Oriental music; he made studies of American Indian, African, Melanesian, Turkish, Japanese, Tunesian, and many other styles, and published samples of their music.[7] In a number of his researches he had the collaboration of Otto Abraham, a physician who was interested in the physiology of music and who widened his scope by studying non-Western musical systems. Hornbostel was for many years director of the archives of the Psychological Institute in Berlin, a large collection of phonograph recordings made in the field. The recordings in these archives were obtained primarily from anthropologists who studied the native inhabitants of the German colonies before World War I; consequently, the Berlin archives were strongest in African and Melanesian musical materials.[8] Under the leadership of Hornbostel, tonometers (instruments for measuring pitch) were installed in the archives and could be taken into the field. In addition to his other achievements, Hornbostel was the teacher of many of the well-known musicologists of today.

Robert Lachmann, another important member of the Berlin group, has worked mainly in Oriental and Near Eastern music.

Erich Fischer did research on South American Indian and Chinese music. Marius Schneider has made elaborate descriptions of primitive and European folk polyphony and of the relationships between Spanish folk music and Arabic music. Miecsyslav Kolinski has studied West African and Canadian Indian music.[9] Herzog, whose work is discussed here later in more detail, first brought to America the methods of the German comparative musicologists.

Two important figures in German ethnomusicology are slightly outside the Berlin group in their interests. Curt Sachs has become the leading specialist in musical instruments. Together with Hornbostel, he devised a scheme for classifying them throughout the world,[10] a task for which he was eminently fitted by his intensive training in the history of art. Even more important that this, however, is his approach to ethnomusicology as a comprehensive music historian. While his colleagues have been content to limit their studies to individual tribes or areas, or at best to either primitive, folk, or Oriental music *in toto,* Sachs has made studies of music the world over, including that of the West. His theories apply to all music and are based on universal samples. The fact that many of them (discussed in later chapters) may be in need of revision is largely due to the fact that at the time of their formulation too little information was available. Sachs, then, has been the most "comparative" of all the comparative musicologists.

Robert Lach, also primarily a music historian, was director of the Phonogramm-Archiv der Akademie der Wissenschaften (archives of non-European music recordings) in Vienna. His main contribution to the study of primitive music is a large collection (numbering well over 2,000) of the songs of non-Slavic tribes living in Russia. These songs, recorded as sung by prisoners of war during World War I, include material from Finno-Ugric, Turk-Tataric, and Caucasian tribes. Lach's theoretical approach differs somewhat from that of the Berlin group: he studies each musical style from the standpoint of its historical position. With an approach similar to that of the evolution-of-culture school of anthropology, Lach believes that all musical styles inevitably go through the same stages of development and that we find them in various stages merely because some progress more rapidly than others.

Finally, although he did not work with primitive music, we should mention the man who first used the methods of the Berlin group of comparative musicologists in studying folk music, Béla Bartók. This great composer, who deserves equal distinction for his scholarly work, contributed much to our knowledge of folk music, especially Balkan and Slavic. A tireless collector and transcriber, he was usually content to give transcriptions and descriptions of musical styles without propounding any far-reaching theories.[11] Evidently he channeled the creative energy that other scholars direct towards theorizing into composition.

As well as compiling the large archives in Berlin and Vienna, the German school founded several series of publications, among which the *Zeitschrift für vergleichende Musikwissenschaft* (Journal of Comparative Musicology) and the *Sammelbände für vergleichende Musikwissenschaft* (collected papers on Comparative Musicology) are the most important. A number of German musicologists also published books on primitive music and comparative musicology as a whole. One of the earliest is Richard Wallaschek's *Anfänge der Tonkunst* (The Origin of the Art of Music), which was followed by Stumpf's *Die Anfänge der Musik* (The Origin of Music). Wallaschek tries to relate simple principles of Western music to those of primitive music; he gives a general picture of regional styles and instruments and reviews theories of the origin of music. Stumpf's book is an outline of primitive music, organized systematically rather than geographically. Sachs and Lach each published a book on the theory and methodology of ethnomusicology, and both give evidence of their background in music history by emphasizing historical problems.[12] Lach's discussion of the relationship between music and language, especially in tone languages, is one of the best of the earlier attempts in this area. Another work worth noting is Robert Lachmann's study of non-European music, which shows depth of background and a broad approach.[13]

In late nineteenth-century America, an awakening of interest in American Indian culture and history led to recognition of the fact that Indian music was gradually disappearing, and in consequence anthropologists began to collect it zealously. One of the first was Theodore Baker, who studied musicology in Leipzig and wrote a general dissertation on North American Indian music.[14] After Baker, however, the study of the continent as a whole was abandoned, to be replaced by attempts to make large collections among individual tribes. Among the early collectors were James Mooney, Alice Fletcher, B. I. Gilman, and Washington Matthews. These people, generally untrained in music (except for Gilman), had as their goal the preservation of Indian music for better qualified scholars of the future. Their work and that of their successors has proven a boon for midcentury ethnomusicologists, who find large collections from extinct tribes very useful. It means that for many years after Indian music has died in its native setting, there will be recorded and transcribed material to be studied.

Among the early American experiments with primitive music should be mentioned those of J. C. Fillmore, a composer. Fillmore, unlike many of his professional colleagues, had a good deal of direct contact with Indian music. He transcribed songs into notation and had them published, in collaboration with Alice Fletcher and Franz Boas. He was also eager to use Indian material in his own compositions, and, through harmonizing it for popular use, he came to the conclusion that there was a latent harmony in the monophonic Indian songs, that a feeling for harmony existed in the natives themselves and had only to be brought out and indicated to them. Fillmore experimented by harmonizing the same song in various ways and presenting the results to Indian informants, who were supposed to express a preference. They almost always agreed in their judgment with Fillmore. Perhaps not realizing that the informants may have been trying to please him by choosing in accordance with subconscious hints on his part, he thought he had made a promising discovery. Fillmore's theory of latent harmony, however, plus the use of Indian material by American composers, did have considerable impact on scholars. To mention only one case, in

1893 Alice Fletcher published *A Study of Omaha Music,* which presents songs of the Omaha Indians in four-part harmonizations, including Fillmore's transcriptions.

In the early twentieth century, a leading American anthropologist, Franz Boas, did much to encourage the study of primitive music among his colleagues and students. Although not formally trained in musicology, Boas was interested in music; he recorded the songs of various North American tribes, notably the Kwakiutl of British Columbia and the Central Eskimo, and transcribed and published their melodies. He realized that music formed an integral part of the ceremonial structure of many Indian religions and believed that these ceremonies should be published with the music included. This practice was employed by the researchers whom he trained and influenced; hence many of their descriptions of American Indian ceremonies and myths contain transcriptions of the songs used therein, which have greatly helped musicologists and anthropologists to integrate the music with its cultural environment.

The most important figures in the development of the study of primitive music in America are Frances Densmore, Helen Roberts, and George Herzog. These three differ considerably in approach and method. Frances Densmore, who was not formally trained as a musicologist or anthropologist, is responsible for the collection and transcription of over 2,000 North American Indian melodies. She has been a tireless recorder, whose aim is to preserve the material for study. Her works, published mainly by the Bureau of American Ethnology in the Smithsonian Institute, include a dozen books with transcriptions and information, mainly on the music of the tribes in the interior of the United States. Her transcriptions are useful and her descriptions of song functions, origins, native singers, instruments, and customs associated with music are valuable. Unfortunately, her analyses are not as reliable. She leans perhaps too heavily on European music theory, and she works in isolation from the methods developed by the Berlin group. Consequently her merit is greatest as collector and transcriber, and as such her contributions to the field are unsurpassed.

Helen Roberts has written a number of excellent detailed studies on primitive music. Most extensive are those of the Copper Eskimo (in collaboration with Diamond Jenness), ancient Hawaiian music, the Shoshonean tribes of Southern California, and musical areas in North America, a significant work which will be discussed in Chapter 9. Her numerous smaller works on North American Indian, New World Negro, and Oceanian music are also important. She has described thoroughly the musical styles of the areas she covered, although she has not attempted to compare the styles of various areas, tribes, and countries. She has reconstructed the histories of some Indian and New World Negro musical styles, but she has not, in general, shared the American interest in relating music to its surrounding culture. She is recognized as one of the most active and prolific workers in the field.

George Herzog is primarily responsible for bringing the methods of the German school to America. Originally a pupil of Hornbostel, he came to America to study anthropology under Boas, and shortly after his arrival he introduced Hornbostel's methods in an article in the *Journal of American Folklore*, in 1928.[15] He did field work among a number of American Indian tribes and in Liberia. Educated as both an ethnomusicologist and an anthropologist, with training in linguistics and folklore, he was well qualified to handle the relationships between music and general culture, language, and oral folk literature; and he stressed these relationships in studies on the function of linguistic tone in Navaho and Jabo music, African drum and horn signaling, Northwest Coast and Salish Indian culture, and music in the thinking of the American Indians.[16] Herzog has also made many comparative studies of various Indian tribes and groups of tribes. Widely acknowledged as a leader of ethnomusicology in America, he has always attempted in his critical review of works by his colleagues to keep the study of primitive music within the traditions of the German school and of American anthropology.

In recent years the links between ethnomusicology and its related disciplines have become stronger. Combining the approaches of ethnomusicology and the psychology of music has produced studies of the relative musical aptitude of different racial groups, such as that of American Negroes and whites by Milton Metfessel.[17] I have applied methods of language study to music and have discovered thereby some promising ways of analyzing music. The application of various theories of anthropology to musical materials has resulted in several new approaches to music, important ones being the American culture area approach, applied to music by Herzog, Roberts, and myself, and the contrasting German *Kulturkreis* (evolution-of-culture) applied by Sachs and Schneider.[18] Gertrude Kurath has studied the correlation of music and dance.[19]

Ethnomusicology today is a large field, with numerous practitioners of many nationalities and trained in differing disciplines. International organization in the field began about 1930, when the Gesellschaft zur Erforschung der Musik des Orients (Society for the Investigation of Oriental Music) was founded, whose organ, the *Zeitschrift für vergleichende Musikwissenschaft*, printed articles on primitive and Oriental music. Following this came the American Society of Comparative Musicology, headed by Charles Seeger, Helen Roberts, and George Herzog, which was active only for a short time. After World War II new efforts were made to organize ethnomusicologists into a society, resulting in the Society for Ethno-Musicology, founded in 1955.

Among the mainstays of the field are the large collections of recordings of native music, ordinarily called archives, which are the chief sources of study. The earliest archives to be assembled, in Berlin, are now relatively defunct as a result of the war, but the archives at Vienna, as well as the large collections in Paris and Brussels, are still in use. In the United States, advances are being made along this line: many institutions are assembling archives, making material available, and exchanging it with each other. The largest American collection of primitive music recordings is in the Department of Anthropology at Indiana University; there are smaller ones at the Library of Congress (which also has a magnificent collection of folk music recordings), Northwestern University, Columbia University, and the universities of California, Michigan, and Washington. Collections of primitive musical instruments may be found in large museums of natural history and ethnology throughout the nation and in many state universities, notably Indiana and Michigan.

The published studies of primitive music can be conveniently divided into five classes: (1) descriptions of musical styles, (2) examinations of the relationship of music to culture, language, dance, and other areas, (3) attempts to determine the history of primitive music, (4) descriptions of musical instruments, and (5) comparisons of musical styles. Most of the completed books and articles can be classified under one or more of these groups; there are additional works of more general theoretical value, but they are relatively rare. About 55 per cent of the published works fall into group (1), 3 per cent into group (2), one per cent into group (3), 35 per cent into group (4), and 6 per cent into group (5). These percentages have a tremendous margin of error and are intended simply to indicate the trends, especially since the areas overlap in many individual cases. But the emphasis on description of styles and instruments is unmistakable, while there have been very few comparative and interdisciplinary studies. This overbalance has no doubt been both unavoidable and beneficial, since obviously it is necessary for material to be made available before it can be elaborated on theoretically. Studies of a comparative and historical nature will probably constitute a far larger percentage in the future than they have in the past.

At the present time, some primitive cultures have been well covered by musicological research while others have been barely touched, and none of the areas have been exhausted in any sense of the word. The most extensive treatment by far has been of the music of American Indians north of Mexico. This area of sparse population (the estimate is about one million in aboriginal times) [20] has had over 4,000 of its songs transcribed and published; there are many works about the music of individual tribes and also several good comparative studies. Even so, of the more than 1,000 tribes in this area, only about eighty have been represented by any musical material at all. We know much less about Middle and South American Indian music, particularly that of the high cultures of Mexico, although some good studies do exist.

African Negro music is relatively well known. However, since it is probably the most stylistically complex of all primitive music, and since Africa has a large population with many tribes, much remains to be done to complete the picture. There are many more kinds of music within each African tribe than within a typical American Indian tribe, and often only one style within a tribal repertory is known. If African Negro music is to be as well documented as North American Indian music, a relatively greater amount of material will have to be furnished.

Our knowledge of Indonesian music is extensive, due primarily to the efforts of Jaap Kunst.[21] Colin McPhee and Manfred Bukofzer have also made important Indonesian studies. There is some information extant on Polynesian music, and, to a lesser degree, on the music of the rest of Oceania. Micronesian music is known through the few but fine studies of Herzog. Certain primitive tribes in Russia, on both sides of the Ural Mountains and in the Caucasus, are relatively well known because of Lach's works; other Asiatic groups, such as the Dravidian tribes of Southern India and the Paleo-Siberian tribes of East Asia, have hardly been touched at all.

At many points the development of the study of primitive music has paralleled that of anthropology at large, as is evidenced by the adherence of many German ethnomusicologists to the *Kulturkreis* school and the adoption by Americans of concepts current in American anthropological theory. This correlation was especially noticeable in the decade after 1940, during which anthropologists became greatly interested in research on acculturation. Works about the impact of Western music on primitive have increased accordingly. One of the most important scholars in this area is Alan P. Merriam, who has analyzed the effect of Western music on that of American Indian and African cultures and has thus contributed to anthropological theory as well as to ethnomusicology.[22]

Although much has already been accomplished and more

material is constantly becoming available, ethnomusicology has barely crossed the threshold of its task, and the need to assemble records is urgent as the music of most primitive cultures is rapidly going out of use. The history of the field has been one of widening interests and increasing collaboration with related areas. Simultaneously, a methodology peculiar to it and suited to its material has been established. Today, students of the Berlin group and its American branch, as well as more independently schooled students, are distributed throughout the world, studying the music of all peoples and countries and attempting to discover more about the essentials of music.

THEORIES AND METHODS OF RESEARCH

Among the various branches of musicology, ethnomusicology has had a distinctive point of view towards research. It has of necessity stressed the importance of objective, unprejudiced investigation, while for the other branches subjective judgment is often unavoidable. In the next few paragraphs, we shall summarize some of the theories and methods of research in this field and touch on some of the problems of the researcher.

The first task is to collect material, to find singers and make recordings. This is rarely easy, for collectors do not readily gain admittance to cultures where music is still alive and functioning, and to obtain valid material from societies which have become acculturated one must locate the few older individuals who remember the songs of the group. Once a singer has been discovered, the techniques of interviewing him and eliciting songs are relatively complex. The collector who is acquainted with the culture and the functions of music therein has a great advantage, for it is often necessary to ask for specific types of songs in order to prod informants. Re-recording the same songs is advisable, so that such things as variation in individual renditions, pitch consistency, and the musical memory of the informants can be investigated later on. The re-recordings should be made using both the original singer and different ones. The process often poses interesting problems. The Plains Indians, for example, are one of the groups which do not ordinarily refer to songs by a title but only by their function — "sun dance song," "rabbit dance song," etc. Since many songs have meaningless texts, this system of nomenclature is necessary; even songs with meaningful words are not identified by text among the natives. However, it means that once a song has been recorded and the investigator wishes to re-record it, he has quite a problem trying to convey to the singer which specific song to sing again. One may ask the singer to repeat a song he has just completed; one may play back his own recording or that of another singer and ask him to reproduce it; one may whistle or hum part of the song to him. All of these methods are weak in that they employ some of the actual musical material which the informant is supposed to recapitulate; they may influence his memory, which one is trying to check, and thus the experiment does not fulfill its purpose. The best procedure is for the investigator to identify the desired song by a symbol, like a name or function, but this is not possible in all cultures. One alternative is to request the informant to repeat at random songs he sang previously, in the hope of identifying them later; another is simply to keep asking him to sing more songs, hoping that eventually he will repeat himself. One should keep a record of the method used, since it may be essential for the subsequent work of a musicologist. Of course, if a musicologist can do his own collecting, so much the better.

Another frequent problem is difficulty in distinguishing one song from another, and for this the investigator must rely on his informant. I have had the experience of supposing that two similar versions of a song were one and the same, and then being corrected by my informant; in another case, my informant identified widely divergent musical materials as variants of the same song. In both situations the song texts were meaningless, so that the differentiations could not have been caused by disparate texts. No generalizations can be made about the solution to this problem. Two renditions considered variants of the same song in one culture may be called different songs in another. It is important to investigate these cultural discrepancies and to quiz informants about their opinions on song variants.

The process of recording monophonic music, particularly if only one performer is involved, presents no special problems, but recording polyphonic music — especially instrumental — is not always simple. If the collector can persuade the performers to give each part separately in addition to giving the entire rendition, he facilitates transcription by a musicologist. When this method is not feasible, the collector may walk about among the players, holding his microphone near the various parts and jotting down the procedure he is following. Another alternative is to record several renditions of the same piece, with the microphone close to a different part each time. Notes on the technique of playing the instruments and, if possible, photographs of them and exact descriptions of their structure should be made available for the transcriber. The ideal medium is sound film, which makes it easy to distinguish what instrument plays what note and to correlate the movements of the players with the sound. For recording music, magnetic tapes are preferable to disks, as they wear much better under constant replaying.

The collector should take down song texts as they are both sung and spoken; there are often differences in pronunciation, as is true of many Western languages (in French, for example, the terminal "e" is sung but not spoken). The pitch pattern of the words may be changed when they are sung, which with a tone language can cause confusion to an investigator, since variation in pitch changes the identity of a word. The collector should include in his notes the function of each song and any information he can glean from informants about its quality, history, composer, alternative ways of performance, etc. Anything the informant can say about the music is worth writing down. But it is usually necessary to prod him with specific questions, since few informants will give unsolicited information. They are not used to volunteering facts; consequently, a great deal depends on the collector's ability to persuade his informants to verbalize about their musical culture.

After the collector has completed his task, it is up to a musicologist to transcribe the recordings into notation — again, a project both difficult and time-consuming. A number of different

transcription schemes have been proposed, some used successfully, others soon abandoned. It was speedily recognized that
primitive music could not be written out in unmodified Western
notation because the intervals employed are frequently different.
Furthermore, the Western system of notation even when applied
to Western cultivated music does not include all that it might.
Many aspects of a performance depend on the artist's familiarity
with musical style, and a musician without this knowledge could
not give acceptable renditions of traditional music even though
he "played the right notes." These aspects of music, largely
omitted in Western notation, are popularly called "interpretation." In notating primitive music, however, our job is not to
devise heuristic devices for the informant or a white performer,
but to indicate exactly what occurred in the execution of the
music. The problems of transcription are indeed considerable.

One suggested solution is to make notations manually on graph
paper, with each square representing a small interval (less than
a minor second) horizontally and a small unit of time vertically.[23]
The same result can be obtained with the aid of an oscillograph,
a machine that records the relative frequency of vibrations by
means of a stylus that writes on graph paper rotating on a drum.
A. M. Jones has used an oscillograph to record African drum
polyphony directly without the mediation of tape recordings.[24]
This method of transcription and most others strive for accuracy
in more minute detail than is common in Western notation. The
system practiced by Frances Densmore and B. I. Gilman, in
contrast, attempts to show just the essential features of a melody
and to deëmphasize details. They have transcribed songs using
only the most important tones therein, in order to delineate
clearly the melodic contour.[25] The method used most widely and
probably most successfully combines with Western notation
some additional symbols designed to clarify special characteristics of primitive music; a list of these symbols may be found on
p. 184.

It is manifestly impossible to notate every musical phenomenon that occurs in a given rendition of a given piece of music.
Minute fluctuations in pitch and slight differences in the rhyth-

mic value of notes are often barely at the threshold of perception. How, then, shall we determine when a transcription is detailed enough to be satisfactory? There are two basic ways of answering this question. These two theories about transcription are not recognized in any official sense, and if you asked an ethnomusicologist which one he subscribed to you would probably not get an answer; but the two points of view exist, nonetheless.

The view held by Herzog and his followers is that all perceptible phenomena should be written down, however minor their place in the music. These scholars might be called the phonetic school, to borrow a term from linguistics: phonetics is the study of linguistic sounds without regard to their significance within a language. Proponents of the phonetic school produce immensely detailed notation; if the transcriber possesses an acutely sensitive ear, the result is a jungle of symbols very difficult to comprehend. Furthermore, because his phenomena are so close to the threshold of perception, the transcriber himself is sometimes unable to decide exactly what the nature of his material is and may vacillate between several interpretations. One is practically never able to sing or play the music by reading from such transcriptions.

To continue the analogy with linguistics, the alternative point of view may be labeled phonemic. Phonemics is the study of speech sounds that are meaningful within a language; it is concerned with rearranging and interpreting the data assembled through phonetic research. The leaders of the phonemic school of music transcription are Hornbostel and Stumpf. This approach calls for more discrimination than does the phonetic, and its adherents take correspondingly greater risks with the validity of their transcriptions. Phonemic notation, logically enough, identifies only those distinctions in a musical style that are significant. In Western cultivated music, for example, quarter tones are not important: they are not indicated in notation nor are they included in Western music theory. But they do occur in singing. In a phonetic transcription they would appear, in a phonemic one they would not. On the other hand, quarter tones are significant in certain styles of Arabic cultivated music, and would have to be indicated in both phonetic and phonemic notations.

The difficult question of which distinctions are significant must usually be settled by the musicologist through analysis of the style he is working with, as performers are rarely able to express any opinion on the matter. When he starts work with a style that is new to him, the transcriber must apply the phonetic approach, setting down every perceptible phenomenon. As he studies variants and perceives the distribution of phenomena, he will gradually learn to discriminate and to interpret all phenomena in the light of the significant ones. Probably no phonemic transcriber will ever be able to eliminate all of the unimportant elements, and as yet there have been no attempts to construct a system of phonemics for a given musical style, as has been done for languages. Despite such flaws, however, phonemic transcriptions are much better suited for publication than phonetic, since they do not force the reader to fight his way through a mass of relatively meaningless detail.

After it has been transcribed and published, the music is available for analysis; and many of the theories and methods of analyzing transcriptions are outlined in the following chapters. Despite a multiplicity of viewpoints, enthomusicologists unanimously agree to the necessity for an objective approach. No musical style is necessarily intelligible to peoples of another culture; sometimes the only features common to differing styles are those by which music is defined. The futility of dogmatic generalization is obvious. The novice in ethnomusicology must above all be on guard against interpreting primitive music in terms of the music to which he has been accustomed all his life; it is so easy to think of unfamiliar intervals as Western ones "sung out of tune." The qualitative equation of all styles is axiomatic to the field. Although every scholar, being human, is bound to have preferences, he is obligated to discard them insofar as possible when he is working, for no valid results are generated by a patronizing attitude.

4

Scale and melody

This chapter and the succeeding ones deal with specific aspects of primitive music. Of course, it is impossible to describe them all exactly, for only a relatively small number are known; so we must confine ourselves to presenting the distribution of various phenomena, describing how musicologists analyze and classify them, and examining some of the theories concerning their origin and function.

CONSTRUCTION AND TYPES OF SCALES

We shall study the relationships between pitches without much consideration of the length, dynamics, and rhythmic function of the notes involved, although we cannot entirely ignore rhythm and form, with which melodic and scale analysis is in some ways intrinsically linked. By melody we mean, of course, the arrangement in succession of the tones in any piece of music; by scale, we mean all of these tones arranged in a way that indicates the relationship between them. An ethnomusicologist constructs a scale out of a primitive melody.[1] This process never occurs in the study of cultivated music, where the scale forms a basis for music that is composed according to its laws; but in primitive music a scale does not exist in the mind of the native musicians, so the musicologist must deduce it from the melodies. If it were possible to construct out of the various scales of one native repertory a system of tones from which all its melodic material issues, the result would compare with the system of tonal relationships which has been generally accepted by Western musicians since approximately 1700, but this has not been accomplished as yet.

How does one go about constructing a scale? Let us follow, step by step, the methods devised by Hornbostel, Herzog, and their colleagues. The first step is to write down all the tones of a song, in either ascending or descending order; the second, to try to find a tonic by examining the melody. An immediate problem arises. What defines the tonic, if not, as in Western music, its spatial relationship to the other tones? In primitive music, the tonic has three main determinants, and at least two are requisite for a tone to be labeled a tonic. They are great frequency and length compared to the other tones, final position in individual sections and phrases, and terminal position in the song. The tone best meeting these qualifications becomes the tonic. If no tone approaches this definition, the final tone is ordinarily so designated. Frequency and final position also determine the other important tones in the song, and the next step in constructing the scale is to assign to each tone a rhythmic designation that symbolizes its importance: the tonic is ordinarily written as a whole note; one or two other important tones are written as half notes; tones of average importance as quarter notes; with rare and weak tones symbolized by eighth notes, sixteenth notes, and grace notes. The other functions of tones within a song should be indicated if possible. For example, if there are several distinct segments in the song, the tones of each segment may be marked by distinctive brackets or lines when the scale is written out. Final tones of the segments may also be specially marked, and the pitch indicated more accurately by the use of the symbols listed on p. 184. It is wise to include in the description of the scale the intervals used in the song, whether or not they are equal in size, and how they are distributed. Example 7 shows a song.

Scales are classified according to the number of tones used, their range, and their intervals. Scholars have tended to emphasize the number of tones, perhaps unjustifiably in view of the fact that primitive scales are seldom fixed or consistent as is the Western diatonic scale. The number of tones is indicated by a Greek numerical prefix plus the suffix "tonic": ditonic describes a two-tone scale, tritonic a three-tone, and so on. Octave duplications of tone are omitted in such designations; for example, a scale having ten tones distributed over two octaves, with each tone appearing in each octave, is pentatonic. This practice is also open to question, for it is based on the belief that primitive people consider that men and women singing the same melody an octave apart are singing in unison. It does not take into account the cultures in which men and women evidently do not sing simultaneously and whose members thus would possibly differentiate between octave and unison singing.[2]

Despite the fact that the known primitive scales are tremendously variegated, including somewhere or other practically all possible tone combinations, there are relatively few scale patterns in common use. Most of the intervals of the scales are fairly similar to those of the tempered scale, although this statement does not imply that tempered intonation is more prevalent than just intonation. Intervals smaller than a tempered minor second are quite rare. One interval widely used in primitive music but foreign to Western is the so-called neutral third, which is roughly between the tempered major and minor thirds. It is interesting to note that all of the scales discussed in the following pages employ rather specialized intervals; each scale uses patterns of intervals peculiar to itself; and in most of them the tones are distributed evenly throughout the scale.

The simplest scales in the world comprise two tones. Although there are a few songs with only one tone, they are usually semi-sung children's rhymes. Example 8 is a typical one. Ditonic scales are characteristic of rudimentary musical styles and simple cultures. The interval is usually a major second or a close approximation of one, less frequently a minor third, and occasionally a major third or minor second. Such simple scales are found throughout the world in isolated regions, and specifically in the music of the Vedda tribe in Ceylon, the tribes of Eastern Siberia, some California Indians, the Fuegians in South America, and tribes on both sides of the Urals. Among these groups, music with the ditonic scale predominates. These scales are, however, found to some extent in practically all repertories the world over, usually constituting only a very small proportion of the scales in any one repertory. The fact that they are distributed so widely and in areas isolated from each other has prompted speculation about their age; songs using them may be the oldest musical material surviving to this day. The ditonic scales are surprisingly uniform: in most cases, the lower tone is the tonic; and the range of intervals employed is very limited. Example 9 presents several songs that have ditonic scales.

Tritonic scales are also found in unsophisticated cultures, and they predominate in more tribal repertories than do ditonic. The two intervals are seldom identical; usually a major second is combined with a minor second or a minor third. In the very few known cases where two thirds are used, they are heterogeneous. Scales consisting of two major seconds have been discovered, but they are likewise quite rare.

The most widely used scale, according to this classification, is the pentatonic. The name "pentatonic scale" is undoubtedly more familiar than the other names that indicate the number of tones in a scale, but it poses a problem to ethnomusicologists nonetheless. There are obviously as many varieties of the five-tone scale as there are possible combinations of intervals, and the pentatonic in its varied forms is the scale most frequently encountered in primitive, folk, and Oriental music throughout the world. It dominates every major musical style except Western cultivated music, where it is subordinate to the far more prevalent diatonic scale.

The most common pentatonic form is composed of major seconds and minor thirds, for example, *c d e g a*, with the tonic occurring on any one of the tones. Scales that lack half steps, like this one, are called anhemitonic. Example 10 is a song of the Menomini tribe of Wisconsin, plus its scale, which is a typical anhemitonic pentatonic scale with an additional grace note. This type is also the main theoretical scale of Chinese cultivated music. Another pentatonic form, characteristic of Japanese cultivated music, consists mainly or entirely of half steps; its intervals are not as standardized as those of the anhemitonic type. There are a few areas where this form dominates the musical styles, for example, the northwest coast of North America. Example 11, a melody of the Uitoto Indians of Brazil, is based on this type of pentatonic scale. A third type is in effect a segment of the diatonic scale: it consists entirely of major and minor seconds. When no octave duplications occur, the scale encompasses a perfect fifth; when they are present, the tones are of necessity distributed unevenly within the octave, leaving an empty perfect fourth as one of the intervals. This last type is usually associated with songs having a rather small range. See Example 12 for an illustration.

Various tetratonic scales exist that are generally similar to the pentatonic ones — in fact, they are often pentatonic with one tone omitted. They are found in the same styles as their corresponding pentatonic scales, but are always used less frequently. This correlation suggests that a rudimentary tone system exists in such cases, with the pentatonic material serving as a basis for songs constructed with a smaller number of tones.

The hexatonic and heptatonic scales in primitive music are almost always parallel to the diatonic scale: the former resemble the hexachords of Guido d'Arezzo; the latter, the modes of Western music. Neither is much use, but a few hexatonic and heptatonic melodies are found in most areas. Only in Negro Africa do they occur frequently, and even there they do not predominate. The intervals employed in heptatonic scales are standardized to an exceptional degree: major seconds are almost always included; minor and augmented seconds are rare, as are any segments of a chromatic scale.

Unlike the theoretical and practical scales of Western music, the scales of primitive music do not have to be acoustically inflexible to be valid. They have, of course, no theoretical basis, since so little music theory is indigenous to primitive cultures. No one knows exactly how certain combinations of intervals came to be used by certain tribes. It is my guess that melodies developed gradually from ditonic to tritonic, and so on.[3] Some tribes may have learned interval arrangements from the Oriental high cultures that did have rather elaborate music theory. However, it is usually futile to attempt to determine whether a given tribe uses Pythagorean or tempered intervals, because the degree of consistency is not great enough and tonometers do not show enough repetition of the same frequencies for any conclusions to be drawn. The range of permissible pitch variation is much greater in primitive than in Western music; singers may deviate farther from the average pitch (we use "average" rather than "standard" since there is not always an ascertainable standard pitch), and such deviation should not be mistaken by researchers for "a bad ear." The number of objectively different pitches that are considered individual tones by native musicians varies from tribe to tribe, as does the concept of accuracy in rendition. It is possible that the amount of variation in pitch allowed in a culture correlates with the size of the intervals used: Arab cultivated music, for example, necessitates even greater accuracy in performance than Western music does, perhaps because it incorporates in its tone system intervals smaller than a second.

Primitive musical instruments are ordinarily tuned in one of two ways, by imitation of another instrument or by the appeal of a visual design. The latter was first pointed out by Charles K. Wead, who made the important discovery that finger holes in wind instruments were usually arranged in some pattern easily perceived by the eye, rather than in a pattern that produced consistent aural results.[4] This visual method of tuning is, of course, confined to those folk and primitive cultures which have no music theory. Wead noticed that the finger holes were usually equidistant; if not, they were arranged in two equidistant groups separated by a blank space. Thus it is hardly surprising that the instrumental scales rarely correspond exactly with the vocal scales occurring in the same tribe. Instead, they are apparently quite isolated phenomena within the cultures possessing them; their development does not seem to have been influenced by the prevalent vocal intervals used in the surrounding areas; and they have a long tradition only in those tribes where an instrument is tuned by copying an older model.

MELODIC RANGE, CONTOUR, AND INTERVALS

One way of characterizing a primitive style is to discover the average range of its songs. The songs with the smallest range belong to the tribes where ditonic and tritonic scales predominate, that is, those in some parts of the Americas, eastern Siberia, Micronesia, Polynesia, southern India, and those near the Urals. The range of their songs is usually a major second, minor third, or a perfect fourth or fifth. The most common range is between a sixth and an octave; this occurs in many American Indian styles and dominates African Negro and much Siberian primitive music. Ranges of over an octave, sometimes as large as two octaves, are found among some American Indians, particularly in the tribes of the North American Great Plains and the Gran Chaco of Brazil and Argentina. While small ranges generally go hand in hand with simple styles, an extraordinarily large range does not imply a complex style. The most sophisticated styles have ranges of about an octave.

A melody is analyzed primarily according to two factors: its melodic movement or contour, and the intervals within it. Melodic movement is a particularly significant factor in scale analysis, one which has been somewhat neglected in favor of the study of scales. In order to determine the contour of a melodic movement, one simply puts on paper a single line that corresponds roughly to the rising and falling melody of the song. Such diagrams are useful in characterizing one particular style, because while the melodic pattern varies from song to song within a style, the diagrams may show an over-all similarity in pattern.

In the discussion of melodic movement, it is helpful to divide songs both into very generalized types and into some rather specialized ones. The general categories are ascending, descending, and undulating movement. It is difficult to draw sharp lines between them, and no infallible determinants have been devised. Hence the investigator must depend largely on his intuitive recognition of the types. Description of descending and ascending movement is unnecessary; undulating means almost equal movement in both directions, using approximately the same intervals for ascent and descent. Extreme undulation that covers a large range and uses large intervals is called pendulum-type melodic movement. Both undulating and pendulum-type melodies usually conclude with a descending progression, as does most primitive music.

Undulating and descending melodies are far more common than ascending ones. Of course, small sections of ascending melody occur within songs that are categorized as either undulating or descending, but we are concerned here with the classification of whole songs, not of short internal progressions. Various theories have been promulgated about the scarcity of ascending melodic movement. One is that breath control is the basic factor, that as a singer loses breath he finds it easiest to sing down. High singing is facilitated by full lungs, so the high pitches are apt to come at the beginning of a song. This theory, however plausible, could only have been applicable to very remote times when singers had not grasped the technique of catching a breath during a song; for in most styles today breath is taken regularly and seems to have little effect on melodic movement. The theory of breath control is also refuted by the fact that towards the end of many songs we find the phenomenon known as "final lengthening," that is, the rhythmic units have increased in size. If singers regularly ran short of breath at the end of a song, this could not take place — the final notes would be hurried.

Because there are only three of these general types, it is impossible to indicate their distribution adequately. Generally speaking, however, descending movement seems to be more prevalent in the New World and Australia, while undulating movement belongs more to the Old World cultures. Each kind appears in both hemispheres, though, and ascending movement is found only in a few isolated areas.

The more specialized types that have been identified characterize musical styles whose melodic progressions are exceptionally homogeneous. The North American Plains Indians possess a cascading type of melodic movement, sometimes also called the "tile" or "terrace" type because of the shape of the graphic transcriptions of their songs. Cascading movement consists of a number of descending phrases, each of which begins on a higher pitch than the last tone of its predecessor. Example 13 is a typical representation of this kind of movement. The contour of its melody is shown in the following diagram.

A melodic contour that resembles an arc is another specialized type. The melody rises and falls in roughly equal amounts, the curve ascending gradually to a climax and then dropping off. A typical arc contour looks like this.

This type is one of those found among the Navaho Indians. Other specialized forms are considered later in the chapter on North American Indian music.

It is important to keep in mind the distinction between the intervals that appear in a scale and those actually occurring in a melody. Large intervals are used in many primitive songs, but they are rarely found in the corresponding scales because of the interpolation of tones of intermediate pitch. In general, seconds and minor thirds are the most common melodic intervals; they almost always carry the bulk of the melodic movement. A few areas are characterized by greater frequency of other intervals, such as major thirds. According to Kolinski, West African music contains a great number of thirds, often in triad formation, in the melodic material.[5] Chains of thirds (both major and minor) moving in the same direction are common everywhere. In some areas of North America, perfect fourths are frequently combined with various kinds of thirds. Among the Navahos, melodic intervals of thirds, fourths, and fifths outnumber seconds, and on the Great Plains, perfect fourths are very frequent. Throughout the world, perfect fourths and fifths and major thirds are the most common intervals next to seconds and minor thirds. Octaves are less used; sixths and sevenths, relatively rare. Intervals larger than an octave are rare except occasionally between adjoining phrases. Repeated tones are common in some styles.

These melodic intervals almost always approximate their Western equivalents, as we would expect from the discussion of intervals occurring in primitive scales. For instance, melodic intervals that bisect the Western perfect and diminished fifths or are smaller than a Western half tone are hardly ever found. (We have already mentioned the only exception to this, the relatively common neutral third.) Tonometric figures evidently give results which challenge this statement; they indicate a large number of melodic intervals absent from nonprimitive music. No doubt the discrepancy exists because the tonometer measures pitches to a point of accuracy far beyond that of the human ear; the *significant* primitive melodic intervals nonetheless correspond closely to Western ones.

The importance of perfect fourths and fifths has often been stated in discussions of musical origins. The simplicity of the acoustic ratios of these intervals and their importance in Western harmony and melody, both folk and cultivated, has been considered evidence of their primary historical position. In primitive music, too, these intervals play a special role. They are relatively common in melodic material, where their intonation is more fixed and conforms more consistently to the acoustical ratios than is true of most other intervals; and in the scales, even where the range exceeds an octave, perfect fourths and fifths figure in an important way. For example, important tones are often separated from each other and from the tonic by fourths or fifths. Individual segments of melodies having large ranges often cover a range of a perfect fourth or fifth. When these intervals are encountered in the scales, they are usually referred to as pentachords and tetrachords, as in ancient Greek terminology.

Curt Sachs has drawn conclusions about the use of intervals and their relationship to general culture patterns and basic psychological types that are, if not convincing, still of great interest.[6] He divides musical material into three main types: logo-genic (word-born), consisting mainly of small intervals; patho-genic (motion-born), consisting mainly of large intervals; and melogenic (music-born), consisting of average-sized intervals. He believed that the first two types are earlier and less sophisticated than the third. The logogenic type, according to his theory, is related to femininity in some sense and is found in matriarchates, cultures dominated by women, while the pathogenic type belongs to patriarchates. Sachs also believed that there was a relationship between music and anatomical types, that small, pygmoid peoples used small intervals and large peoples, large ones. Similarly, the size of the dance steps of a tribe was supposed to corre-late with the size of their musical intervals. General cultural traits were also reflected in music, Sachs concluded; warlike tribes tended to use large intervals and peace-loving peoples smaller ones.

Let us proceed to a brief critique of Sachs's theories, since they are widely known and accepted and certainly deserve com-mentary. There seems to be a considerable amount or correlation between the size of dance steps and of musical intervals. Con-cerning the relationship between matriarchates, small intervals, and peace-loving peoples, there is apparently some correlation, but there are also many exceptions, and the basic concepts of the theory should be examined. Probably most American anthro-pologists would not accept Sachs's concept of matriarchate. He generally assumes that in tribes that reckon descent through the female hereditary line women are more important. This assump-tion may be refuted by examples from many cultures. Further-more, even where women are obviously the leaders in most fields, they are not always the leaders in musical activity. Among the Iroquois of the eastern United States, women hold more power than in almost any other culture; they own all property, have power to assign men work, and even elect the governing council — whose members, to be sure, are men.[7] Although this tribe is the closest to a complete matriarchate we have been able to discover, it runs counter to Sachs's theory by being warlike to a considerable degree, and the intervals of the songs are average or larger than average.

Such refutations may be caused by his failure to take sufficient account of past contact between various tribes. For example, in an area where peaceful tribes are constantly harassed by belligerent neighbors, the association between them is likely to encourage similar musical styles, and if a warlike tribe conquers another, its musical style will probably be accepted by the vanquished. Such exchanging of musical material has doubtless been in progress for centuries and quite possibly has had more influence on stylistic development than the basic psychological types described by Sachs. Yet since Sachs does not claim to take historical movements into consideration, but theorizes about hypothetically isolated primitive communities, his conclusions may well be applicable to a historical period long past. Of course, since they require experimental evidence for proof, it is highly unlikely that they will ever be entirely validated.

OTHER CHARACTERISTICS OF PRIMITIVE MELODIES

Transposition of whole songs is also important in analyzing melodic material. The use of the same songs at various pitches, separated by either small or large intervals, is found in a number of primitive styles. Transposition to a small interval like a second is common in some North American Indian styles, although here the transpositions are not always accurate and frequently one constitutes a variation on the other. Example 15, from a Peyote song is typical of a song transposed to a small interval. Transposition of songs to pitches a fourth, fifth, or even an octave away from the original are usually more exact and also more common. Transposition down a fourth or fifth is often encountered in North American Indian music on the Great Plains and in the music of some Finno-Ugric tribes in Russia. Example 14 is a Cheremis song in two sections, the second being a version of the first, transposed down a fifth. Transposition up an octave is found in the music of some California Indian tribes (see the discussion of the rise, p. 173).

Ornamentation of the melodic line by various kinds of grace notes, occasional trills, mordents, and other figures composed of short notes and contrasting in dynamics with the more organic material is found in many primitive styles. Lach attempted in his large study *Entwicklungsgeschichte der ornamentalen Melopoeie* to trace throughout the world the development of ornamentation from material that was originally organic. He concluded, in the main, that all ornamentation derived from organic material, that progressions originally primary in nature had shriveled up, as it were, and become subsidiary to the basic melodic line. His conclusions have been substantiated at least in part by musical evidence.

Broadly speaking, ornamentation falls into two categories according to the relationship of its tones to those of the melody proper. In some music the ornamental tones fit in with the scale of the melody as a whole, no additional ones being used. This type supports the Lach hypothesis particularly well. But in other cases ornamental tones are used to fill in larger melodic intervals, and these ornaments (a typical one is the *pien* in Chinese music) appear to be of nonorganic origin. It is possible, in fact, that for such melodies the reverse of Lach's theory might hold true, for could it not be that scales of originally few tones tended to expand by creating unimportant ornamental tones outside of the scale, and then gradually giving them the status of regular tones? We may infer that the process worked both ways: some ornamental material grew out of tones originally organic, while some organic tones developed from initially ornamental material as the scale expanded. Example 16 shows typical ornamentation in primitive music, with the ornaments represented by small or crossed notes.

Ornamentation is often closely related to what we call sound production or vocal technique. Since most primitive music, statistically speaking, is vocal or at least partly vocal, sound production refers primarily to music produced by the human voice. Primitive singing often sounds very different from Western cultivated singing and even from our popular and folk songs. Primitive people sing with specialized techniques, some of which may be based on racial differences. The key to many of the peculiar qualities of primitive singing is tension of the vocal chords — generally speaking, most primitive singers use a tenser vocal technique than we are accustomed to, although there are exceptions, like the Yuman tribes of western Arizona.[8] The tensest known technique was found among some North and South American Indian tribes, whose method of sound production gives rise to a great deal of ornamentation: accented ornamental tones, pulsations that imply considerable dynamic contrast, and falsetto. According to Herzog, ornamentation has caused scale expansion among these tribes.[9]

The African Negroes sing generally with a tense, slightly hoarse-sounding vocal technique, which is also used by some American Negro singers and is evidently partially responsible for the strange vocal and instrumental sound production in early New Orleans jazz. Sometimes unusual vocal technique, like Alpine yodeling, can be traced to the attempt of singers to imitate instruments. In many parts of Negro Africa, singers alternate falsetto with ordinary tone production to produce a sound reminiscent of yodeling.[10] The Navaho Indians use falsetto in a clear, nonornamented way. Other specialized forms of sound production exist which are characteristic of individual areas.

We have already seen that the instrumental scales of a tribe tend to differ radically from its vocal scales, so it is hardly surprising to find that the melodic techniques for instrumental music have developed separately from those for vocal songs. They are of course limited by the technical possibilities of the instruments and are often very restricted and stereotyped. For example, the musical bow is capable only of a relatively small range, unless it is accompanied by the mouth as a resonator. Example 17 is characteristic of musical bow material in South Africa. It is in sharp contrast to the vocal style of this area, which tends to have large intervals and ranges.

Flute melodies in North American Indian music differ typically from the vocal styles used by the same tribes. In some areas, notably the Plains, the melodic movement of most songs is descending and cascading, while flute melodies tend to have a relatively undulating movement, perhaps because flute technique has developed by playful manipulation over the finger holes in both directions. Example 18 is a typical flute song. This style, it is interesting to note, has carried over into love songs, many of which are intended to be either sung or played on the flute. In general, however, the independence of vocal and instrumental styles within the same repertory must be stressed; it is one of the striking parallels between primitive and cultivated musical styles.

THEORY OF TONAL ORGANIZATION

Finally, we should discuss the possibility of the presence in primitive music of a concept common in Western music theory, tonality. While it is relatively easy to define a scale, to differentiate between a scale used in an individual song and a tone system used as the basis for an entire repertory of musical pieces is a problem. In vocal music, it is exceedingly difficult to arrive at a clear conception of a tone system; the various tonal limitations of individual instruments make solution easier for instrumental music. Investigators have ordinarily made a practice of indicating the presence of tonality in primitive music if they intuitively sensed any similarity therein to the tonality of Western music; if one could "feel" tonality, that sufficed. Verification by native informants is manifestly impossible, since they cannot verbalize on such topics, and the solution to this problem has been delayed by the unfounded assumption that tonality was lacking in primitive music if a Western auditor failed to sense it.

Let us substitute for the much used and misused word "tonality" the phrase "tonal organization," and let us define it tentatively as the totality of the relationships between all the tones in a particular piece of music. One formulates the tonal organization by tabulating the various relationships, frequencies, orders of succession, etc., and by this process one finds the degree of importance of tones, intervals (of melodies and scales), and recurring formulas and motifs. A brief description of the tonal organization of a piece should indicate the tonic and show whether the tonic changes in the course of the piece (modulation), whether other important tones function temporarily as the tonic, and whether there are any specialized relationships, leading tones, or other characteristic progressions.

SUMMARY

The most frequently used scale is some form of the pentatonic, followed by tetratonic and hexatonic. Tritonic, heptatonic, and ditonic scales are rarer, and limited in their distribution. In general, simplicity of scale coincides with general simplicity of musical style, and complexity of scale with sophistication of style. Ornamentation is in many musical cultures dependent largely on the method of sound production, especially in vocal music; certain types of vocal technique almost automatically produce ornaments, while others do not; and the amount of ornamentation correlates to some extent with the amount of vocal tension. While few generalizations can be made contrasting primitive music as a whole with Western, it is dangerous to use the methodology of European music theory to analyze primitive styles without some qualifications. The melodic and scale material of primitive music is actually not elemental but often highly complex. Vocal technique, intentional distortions of the voice, and the construction of musical instruments, all play a large part in determining melodic style. Some theories about the origin of melodies correlate them with basic psychological types, cultural types, or physical types; others, perhaps more realistic and taking into account historical migration and interaction, refer to geographic movements of peoples and to contact between various primitive cultures.

5

Rhythm and form

A discussion of rhythm, that rather elusive but primary element in music, hinges partly on its definition. Curt Sachs, in his recent book *Rhythm and Tempo*, struggles with this problem and concludes that any workable definition can be formulated only with the utmost difficulty. He summarizes the theories of the origin and background of rhythm, considers how the term is used in poetry and the fine arts and the problems arising from this multiple use, and gives a considerable amount of detailed information about the rhythmic characteristics of primitive music. Instead, however, of reviewing all of the past definitions of rhythm or attempting a logically consistent definition here, let us simply give a working definition that will be used in describing the rhythmic elements of primitive musical styles. Rhythm, in this discipline, means movement in time.

The two predominant aspects of rhythm are dynamic and durational contrast. The fact that rhythm takes this two-dimensional form has probably been the root of the difficulty in defining and recognizing rhythm. Furthermore, it has four main facets, which are hierarchical and necessary for the identification of time relationships at various levels. The first is tempo: the relative speed of a beat, movement, or pulse that is basic to an entire section of music and that usually remains intact for considerable lengths of time. The second facet is the study of the durational values of tones: their number, relationship, and relative frequency. The third is meter, most simply defined as the recurrence of stressed points in contrast to unstressed ones. The fourth is the time relationship between larger sections: their patterns of durational values and metric units, in short, the over-all design of the various interrelationships of stress and length. All of these terms are useful in describing and differentiating between primitive styles.

Rhythm is in some ways the most basic musical principle. For this reason, the theory has been advanced that rhythm appeared before any of the other musical phenomena. It is indeed possible to have rhythm (in the form of drumming, for example) without any melody, while melodic material without some kind of rhythmic organization is inconceivable. But this theory is challenged by the fact that only fairly complex musical cultures, like those of Negro Africa, have rhythmic manifestations without melody; the simplest musical styles, like those of the Vedda, the Modoc and Klamath of California, and the Fuegians, have no solo drums or other solo percussive music. Consequently we must assume that rhythmic organization came into being no earlier than melody and that the two have always been complementary.

A number of theories that deal with rhythm in primitive culture and its origin are of interest in this context. We do not plan to discuss here all the theories on the origin and nature of rhythm, only those relevant to the study of primitive music. One of the earliest was the principle of *Vierhebigkeit* (roughly translated, "integrity of the number four"), propounded by Hugo Riemann.[1] According to this theory, which is based on the fundamentally binary nature of human physiology and anatomy (e.g., inhalation-exhalation and bilateral symmetry), all music can ultimately be divided into quadruple meter. Quadruple meter was chosen instead of duple because of the four chambers of the heart. Riemann attempted to reorganize primitive melodies using quadruple meter. He had little success, for *Vierhebigkeit* contradicts one of the best known and most widely recognized characteristics of primitive music: its frequently asymmetrical and irregular structure.

Another theory concerned with the origin of music was propounded by Carl Bücher in his book *Arbeit und Rhythmus*. Bücher, an economist, believed that rhythm appeared in music as the result of group work carried on rhythmically, and that rhythmic work was adopted when people recognized its superior efficiency compared to work done by isolated individuals. Bücher discovered that the Western folk repertory as well as some primitive ones contained a number of work songs, and he concluded that this must have been the first type of song. However, he did not realize that the simplest cultures in the world do not have work songs, and that even when they work in groups they do not recognize rhythmic efficiency. Indeed, it is only in quite sophisticated cultures that the advantages of rhythmic work, and specifically singing to accompany work, have been discovered. On examination, Bücher's theory appears unsubstantiated; apparently its opposite is closer to the truth.

RHYTHMIC ORGANIZATION

A great many works in ethnomusicology display some confusion in describing the general assumptions about the relative complexity or simplicity of primitive musical rhythm. This is especially true of books written three or more decades ago. One school of thought assumes that simple rhythmic organization, exemplified by four-four time, is common in primitive music. Another considers this simple metric division too sophisticated to be indigenous to any primitive style and thus ascribe its presence, regardless of locale, to Western influence. This school of thought expects primitive music to have no inherent rhythmic organization whatsoever, an unfounded assumption because, as we shall see, primitive music that seems to lack organization usually has a rhythmic structure so complex that it is difficult to perceive. Consequently, scholars who characterize the rhythm of primitive music either as very simple or as lacking in organization are creating insoluble problems for themselves. The truth is far different and is compatible with most of what we have already said about primitive music: the rhythmic forms are quite varied; some are exceedingly simple, while others are probably more complex than anything in Western music. Herzog describes the prevailing asymmetry of primitive rhythm as its most conspicuous characteristic.[2] This exists, to be sure, but there are a great many types of asymmetry, and we cannot avoid concluding that the various primitive styles incorporate approximately equal shares of these types. Perhaps this very profusion causes the difficulty that scholars have had in describing rhythm and in formulating theories about it. Or the opposite may be true: because no acceptable theory has been proposed, the world of musical rhythm seems to be a jungle of unrelated elements, a vast array of forms without organization, a labyrinth of diverse materials that defy categorization. Nonetheless, we shall attempt to analyze some of the more common rhythmic forms of primitive styles, in accordance with our working definition of rhythm as movement in time.

Tempo. Few generalizations can be made about tempo; it varies so, and in instrumental music is largely determined by mechanical limitations. Changes of tempo during an individual piece occur in some of the American Indian styles, especially the most complex ones, but they are rare elsewhere. Gradual acceleration of tempo during a piece is found in many styles. However, strict adherence to a given tempo is also common, particularly in African Negro music, where drumming in complex designs frequently serves as an accompaniment. Music in which the only rhythmic manifestation is a pulse — that is, even beats without dynamic differentiation — is rare. Some of the drum accompaniments of North and South American Indian songs may fall in this category, but neither solo drumming nor melodic material ever do.

Durational values. In describing a melody, the ethnomusicologist should list the number of durational values included — quarter notes, eighth notes, etc. — and their frequency. This information is another means of characterizing and comparing styles. Some styles use only a few durational values — perhaps two — in an individual song, while others use five or six. Still other styles use many durational values but only two or three frequently. It is also helpful to give in numerical ratios the relative frequency of the values used. Thus the Peyote songs described on pages 17–18 use only two durational values, which always bear the relationship of 1:2 (e.g., eighth notes appear half as often as quarter notes). Example 19 is a song of the Georgians in the Caucasus, using seven durational values.

In most African Negro music, which as we have seen has the reputation of being very sophisticated rhythmically, relatively few durational values are found but the ratios among them are often complicated. For example, take the bit of rhythmic polyphony of the Ibo in Example 20. It is performed by a solo singer who drums at the same time. The drum and the voice taken separately have only two durational values apiece, with the ratio of 1:2, but the ratios of the four taken together are 9:10:18:20. For the Western listener this complexity is infinitely more bewildering than a song like Example 19, with its seven durational values.

It is of considerable interest to find that in each primitive style the number of durational values in every song is approximately the same. Indeed, one can characterize the rhythm of a particular style simply by giving the number of values and the predominant ratios. This situation is in sharp contrast to Western art music, where individual composers display great rhythmic variation.

Meter. The irregularity of stress patterns characteristic of primitive music might lead us to believe that most of it is heterometric, that is, that the meter changes during a given piece of music. A rough sampling reveals that approximately 60 per cent of all primitive musical materials are indeed heterometric. It is often difficult to determine meter solely on the basis of stress patterns; examination of recurrent sequences of durational values as well as of melodic patterns may aid in identifying metric units.

Consistent use of isometric patterns (those without change in meter during the course of the music) occurs frequently only in African Negro music, not in the music of preliterate cultures in any other area of comparable size. This phenomenon suggests some relationship between African Negro and Western music, particularly Western European folk music, a topic to be discussed further in Chapter 9. At any rate, a great deal of isometric material may have assumed this form because of repeated rhythmic patterns in a percussive accompaniment. In African Negro music the drums have rhythmic designs of their own and thus sometimes seem to regulate the rhythmic designs in the melody, while in American Indian music, which tends to be heterometric, drumming rarely has any pattern other than a steady pulse. Where complex percussive rhythmic designs do exist in America, as on the North Pacific Coast, there are an unusually large number of isometric songs. It would seem that isometric melodies, as they occur in Africa and in European folk songs, are a rather specialized form, dependent in most areas on the development of some music theory. Much more widespread in the world and apparently more generalized in their development are the heterometric patterns, whose growth may have been subject to other laws, such as the aesthetic preferences that have influenced the speech and other aspects of any given culture. Indeed, the origin of isometric patterns in music seems to be related to the beginning of meter in poetry, a fact that may be of great significance in ethnomusicology. It is likely that in Europe, at least, metric poetry preceded isometric music and that in consequence the rhythmic organization of European folk music is very specialized and must be accepted as a deviation from the universal norm.

Final lengthening. One rhythmic feature of musical units that is present in the majority of all primitive material is final lengthening.[3] Towards the end of a section, phrase, or entire piece of music, all the rhythmic units tend to increase in length. Example 21 illustrates final lengthening at various levels: the end of each phrase is marked by a long note, the end of the song by a longer one yet. As a general rule, also, long notes are more likely to appear near the end of a song than near its beginning, and the same is true of longer measures (i.e., longer spans between stress points). Because of the lengthening of these smaller rhythmic units, the larger design patterns also increase in length. Final lengthening, however, is not a universal characteristic; in some styles, and in many compositions of most styles, shortened units hold the terminal position.

Isorhythmic structure. The presence of isorhythmic material, i.e., repeated series of durational values, in primitive music is viewed with evident surprise by some scholars, including Curt Sachs.[4] The reason why is not clear, in view of the fact that simple repetition of material has apparently been thought fundamental in the development of music. Isorhythmic tendencies are found in many primitive styles of North America, among other areas. The simple repetition of a rhythmic pattern in a song is very common, although this pattern is rarely repeated throughout an entire piece of music. Even where the isorhythmic unit remains constant until the end of the song, it usually gives way to final lengthening. Further modifications of absolute isorhythmic structure are caused by the breaking of a single note into two notes and by similar changes, which are often due to textual considerations. Example 22 is typical of the kind of isorhythmic song found among some of the American Indian tribes. Example 23 from the Cheremis has a similar isorhythmic construction; in this case the rhythm is evidently related to the structure of the text (not reproduced here) — each two-measure group corresponds to a textual phrase.

Isorhythmic structure serves as a unifying factor in a song form. It seems to be capable of replacing other unifying factors, such as isometric structure or repeated melodic sections. The Menomini Indians of the Great Lakes area, for example, have a large number of isorhythmic songs but very few recurring repeated sections in their song forms. Among the neighboring Ojibwa Indians, where the musical style is otherwise similar to that of the Menomini, there are fewer isorhythmic songs and more songs with recurring sections. The isorhythmic songs of the Menomini are also less apt to have repeated sections than are their songs characterized by less restricted rhythmic organization.

Rhythmic polyphony. Our final consideration here is the use of several rhythmic structures simultaneously, or rhythmic polyphony. While in a great deal of primitive part music several voices have notes of differing durational value, such music should not be considered rhythmic polyphony in the true sense of the word. True polyphony implies divergency of stress patterns, or metric units, in the various parts. Simple disagreement of durational values does not constitute rhythmic polyphony but could be labeled counterpoint. Examples of rhythmic polyphony are found in some areas having complex musical styles, such as Negro Africa, Melanesia, and places in Central Asia that have been influenced by Indian cultivated music. Example 24, a piece for four drums, shows true rhythmic polyphony.

CLASSIFICATIONS OF FORM

The study of form, the interaction between melody and rhythm and the interrelationship of identifiable sections, hinges on several possible methods of classification. The first method gives the relationship between a musical section and its successors in a given piece. There are three main relationships, and they can be used to determine the form of individual songs and even to characterize styles. The first form is iterative, the immediate repetition (possibly with some variation) of a section; the second is reverting, the repetition of material introduced earlier in the song; and the third is progressive, moving on to completely new material.[5] More than one of these relationships may appear in a song — to be sure, progression is present to an extent in every piece of music. Nonetheless, the three forms are useful in ethnomusicological description. A musical style consisting primarily of short repeated sections, like some found in Negro Africa, may be classified as iterative; a style in which patterns like ABCA or ABBA play a major role, such as Hungarian folk music, may be classified as primarily reverting.

Furthermore, it is useful to classify styles according to the prevalence and length of repeated sections. When a long section or the whole piece is repeated, the structure is called strophic. Sometimes new text is provided for each strophe (repeated musical section), and sometimes the same text, whether meaningful or not, accompanies the same strophe whenever it recurs. The latter type of strophic song occurs frequently in many North American Indian styles. Styles lacking large-scale repetition are called through-composed, to borrow a term from European art music, where it indicates that each of a number of textual stanzas is sung to a different musical section. The term in primitive music means only that there is no repetition of the entire piece or of very large portions thereof. Primitive strophic songs usually have a fixed number of repetitions, and they are generally shorter than through-composed pieces. A third form consists of one short motif, repeated many times, that is not long enough to be considered a strophe; we shall term it litany-type, following the terminology of Friedrich Gennrich and Robert Lach.[6] Litany-type structure differs from strophic in that each strophe of the latter contains many small sections, whereas the former usually consists of only one short phrase that is reiterated throughout.

Strophic form. Strophic form is probably the most common one throughout the realm of primitive music. There are many types: with refrains, with antiphonal or polyphonic techniques, and with reverting, iterative, or progressive elements predominating. The area of greatest frequency is that which stretches from the Ural Mountains across Siberia and into the New World. Strophic is also the main type of form in European folk music. Strophes are characteristically sectional: they may be divided into a number of sections, between three and ten on the average. The relationship between the various sections is interesting. It is relatively rare for a strophe to be progressive throughout. Broadly speaking, the strophic forms can be divided into two groups: those with strophes containing iteration, variation, and transposition of sections; and those with strophes that are primarily reverting. The reverting strophes are the main type in Western European strophic folk songs. They may often be schematized as A B C A or A A B A. Example 25, whose pattern is A A B A B, is typical of the reverting strophic forms. The iterative and transposing strophic forms are somewhat more complex, occurring in more variations. The American Plains and Great Basin Indians have "Ghost Dance songs" (see pp. 108–109 for a description) in which each section of the strophe is repeated once. In these strophes, according to Herzog, forms like A A B B C C are typical (see Example 26), and the repetitions do not vary much from the original sections.[7] Iterative strophes with more variation are common elsewhere, on the Northwest Coast of North America, for example, and in Negro Africa, where variation is a conspicuous element in the melodic structure.

Transposition of sections of strophes is found in many styles. The section is usually transposed to a pitch removed by a fourth, fifth, octave, or a similarly large interval. One of the simplest strophes of this type consists of the first phrase and its transposition up or down a perfect fifth. It is common in the music of some Russian tribes, as well as in Hungarian folk music. In Example 27, a song of the Mongolians, measures 5 and 6 are the same as measures 2 and 3, transposed down a fifth. Transposition to large intervals is common in the areas inhabited primarily by Mongoloid peoples, whose songs are characterized by large melodic intervals and songs. The sequence, which is transposition of a section to a pitch removed by a short interval — usually a second, occurs infrequently and in those styles having diatonic-like scales. The West African Negroes sing in sequences, as is shown by Example 28. This song of the Ibo in Nigeria may possibly exhibit European influence, but the form of transposition is evidently native. The second measure is a downward transposition of the first.

American Indian music also includes a great deal of transposition of sections within strophes. One of the simplest varieties can be seen in Example 29, a song of the Arapaho, where the initial phrase is followed by a contrasting one and then reappears an octave lower. The Plains Indians use quite elaborate transpositions; various transposed sections will occur during the same song, while other unifying elements are rarely used. One Pawnee song, for example, contains six expositions of one phrase, transposed to various intervals, but only two phrases of contrasting material. Its transpositions are consistently to a perfect fifth: the first transposition to a fifth is transposed again a fifth lower, so that the third rendition is pitched a major ninth below the first. This song has the following form: A^1 A^1 A^1 (fifth) B A^2 (fifth) A^1 (fifth) A^3 (major ninth) B. Example 30, an Arapaho song, has this pattern: A^1 A^2 (major second) A^2 (major second) B^1 A^3 (major second) A^3 (major second) A^4 (major sixth) A^5 (minor seventh) B^2 (fourth) A^6 (octave) B^3 (octave).

In general, the interval used in transposition correlates with the kind of scale and the tonal organization of the style. Transposition is a very widespread technique of formal development and, in some styles, is one of the major characteristics.

Through-composed form. Through-composed form is less common than strophic. It too tends to lean on various types of repetition as the main device for unifying the piece; entirely progressive material is rare. Through-composed songs often coincide with a recitative-like manner of performance: one in which the meter is usually complex but the interrelationship and number of durational values are simple, and in which the melody and rhythm of speech are prominent. Such is the case in many songs of the Eskimos, like Example 32. The recurrence of a short motif in a form that is predominantly through-composed is frequent among some Indian tribes of the North Pacific Coast. Although due to the inherent nature of the form these motifs are often difficult to isolate, they do serve as a unifying device. At the end of Example 31, a through-composed song of the Tsimshian, the motifs are transcribed separately. Finally, there is a type of through-composed form that is essentially an outgrowth of litany-type; the individual repeated phrase characteristic of the latter is modified by the intrusion of new elements. This type is found among the North American Indians in California and Western Arizona, the so-called Yuman-speaking tribes.[8]

Litany-type form. Litany-type form is found in a number of variations in Negro Africa and Central Asia, as well as among primitive tribes in Russia, and it is present to a small extent in the eastern part of the United States among some of the Indians of the Eastern Woodlands and southeastern culture areas. In many ways, it is the simplest form found in primitive music. It is the main form of the simplest styles in the world, those characterized by ditonic and tritonic scales and small range. It occurs both with and without variations. Completely iterative litany-type songs are found among some tribes in Central Asia and on both sides of the Urals, especially the Finno-Ugric, the Permiak, and the Ostiak. Example 33 illustrates the type: a single short phrase is repeated with little or no variation. A small amount of variation is found in the two sections of a Vedda song given in Example 10. Occasionally litany-type is used in conjunction with antiphonal or responsorial techniques; and a great deal of this type of variation in basically litany-type music occurs in Negro Africa. In Example 2, which is responsorial, the leader varies his part considerably while the choral part remains relatively unchanged. This type of variation between choral and solo repetition is typical of African Negro music; the amount of variation in the leader's part distinguishes the African technique from similar ones used in North America and in European folk singing.

A form closely related to litany-type and found in the same areas begins with progressive material and then lapses into itera-tive treatment of a single stanza. This type is common among the Cheremis and is thought by Lach to be a modification, influenced by the more complex Tataric music, of the litany-type used by some of the Finno-Ugric neighbors of the Cheremis.[9] Example 34 is typical. A similar form from Equatorial Africa is illustrated in Example 35, where it has been modified by the introduction of polyphonic elements.

Antiphonal and responsorial form, as we have seen, is also related to litany-type. Any of the kinds of form we have dis-cussed may be associated with antiphonal or responsorial tech-niques, but in actual fact they usually occur in simple forms in most primitive cultures. Most common is material in which the leader or the first chorus presents a single phrase that is repeated by the answering group or individual. In African Negro music, variation by one group — usually the first — is the rule, result-ing in a form that may be schematized as A^1 A A^2 A A^3 A, etc. Another simple type of antiphony has different materials for each part, making the scheme A B A B A B, sometimes with variations. This form is found in African Negro music, where variation by one of the groups is common, and in the Eastern part of North America, where variation is less frequently en-countered. Example 36 from the Shawnee Indians has the scheme A A A A B B B B, etc.

Litany-type and the two modifications of it just discussed are the simplest forms in existence. They are widely distributed and are found in areas of both simple and complex musical style. It is probable that litany-type developed first. The modified litany-type used by the Finno-Ugric may have come into being because melody was more important than polyphony in their culture. In areas where polyphony was, for some unknown reason, at more of a premium than melodic complexity, antiphonal techniques were incorporated with the simple litany-type form. Thus we may postulate litany-type as one of the earliest forms in the world, one that has given rise to other forms that are more complex but essentially repetitive.

The Rise. Most forms in primitive music can be classified as strophic, through-composed, or litany-type, but there are a few forms which do not fall easily into these categories. One of the most prevalent is the rise, which combines elements from all three. A rise is a section of a song that is pitched high, a kind of musical plateau, and often contrasts with the surrounding material. The non-rise portion of a song frequently consists of one short section repeated many times; this is sporadically interrupted by the rise, so that a typical pattern would be A A A A A rise A A A rise, etc. The number of repetitions is not usually fixed, so we cannot designate the form strophic.

THE MEANING OF "COMPLEXITY"

We have mentioned the relative complexity of primitive forms a number of times, but we have not hitherto defined complexity. It is very difficult to delineate completely, and most judgments of relative complexity in the past have been based on intuition. However, we can make a few definite statements. The number of identifiable sections of a form is one determinant, and another is the number of relationships between them. A form having progressive, iterative, and reverting elements is more complex than a form having one of these elements strongly pronounced. Hence the more complex a form is, the harder it is to classify according to the categories we have examined in this chapter. To extend this observation, if we were to try to classify all the forms of

Western art music used during one historical period since the Renaissance, we would no doubt be at a loss to find a single prevailing trait. In medieval and primitive music it is easier to characterize the forms of an entire style, and those styles intuitively felt to be simplest are usually the easiest to classify concretely. For example, the forms used by the Great Basin Indians, who have one of the simplest styles in the New World, can be classified as primarily iterative because each individual phrase in most of their music is repeated. On the other hand, the style of the Northwest Coast Indians, which has more complicated melodies, scales, and rhythms, cannot be easily characterized because it uses progressive, iterative, and reverting elements and includes both through-composed and strophic forms.

It is probable that the complex forms in primitive music have expanded gradually from the simple ones. Out of the rather homogeneous forms of the simplest styles, the more heterogeneous ones in the complex styles have grown; and in Western cultivated music we find a forest of differing forms, each composition having its individual sections interrelated in a manner not duplicated elsewhere.

OTHER ASPECTS OF FORM

Length. There is a certain amount of conformity in the length of primitive songs. Most primitive pieces are short, the average duration of a song being about half a minute. The songs with the simplest and shortest forms sometimes last no longer than ten seconds, while the longest ones, among which those of the Pueblo Indians are foremost, sometimes take as long as two minutes to complete a single strophe. The amount of time involved correlates approximately with the complexity of the scale and the melody, but not necessarily with that of other features like rhythm and polyphony.

The few long pieces occur in two forms. The first is the song series, which is found in a number of cultures, particularly in North America and Polynesia.[10] A succession of many songs, sometimes more than one hundred, is sung in a particular order as an accompaniment to a spoken myth or a ceremony. Organization within the individual songs in these series certainly exists, but there is little musical organization in the series as a whole. Often, however, all the songs of a particular series have the same style and are related by specific melodic formulas, cadences, or calls. Native informants express the feeling that the songs belong to their series and should be performed in a particular order, so it seems legitimate in one sense to consider this phenomenon a musical composition in itself. The second long musical form is a litany-type repeated many hundreds of times. It is usually confined to instrumental music; for example, the xylophone players at the West African markets play variations of one phrase for hours. As in the song series, the short form is the basic one (in this case, the motif of the litany-type), and the long form has no over-all organization. Thus we find that time duration is one of the most striking differentials between primitive music and the cultivated music dramas and orchestral pieces of the West and the Orient.

Cadences. There are in each style certain places during a song where the form is more stable and the entire musical material relatively more homogeneous than elsewhere. The most common is the cadence, which is stereotyped in many cultures. The stereotyped cadence of eighteenth and early nineteenth century art music, the progression from the dominant to the tonic, is familiar to all Western listeners, and many primitive styles use similar cadential formulas. We have already seen that practically all the Peyote songs end with four long even notes on the tonic, a formula with both rhythmic and melodic significance. In most styles, however, the cadential formulas assume variant forms and are united by only one common feature, such as a particular rhythm or sequence of intervals. For example, among the Plains Indians the final melodic interval is likely to be a descending perfect fourth or minor third, followed by a number of repetitions of the final tone, of varying durations. On Uvea, an island in Polynesia, Burrows discovered three kinds of cadence: a downward glissando, shouts, and a prolonged tone a perfect fourth below the tonic.[11] In some styles songs with different functions have different cadences. Formulas restricted to the beginning and ending of songs are common in many areas, and sometimes they also serve to identify the function of a song for native listeners.

Shouts. Shouting before and after a song is common throughout the world, but whether it should be classified as part of the musical form is debatable. Stylized shouts that agree with the musical material in scale and rhythm may be considered part of the form; they are less widely distributed than nonmusical shouts, and are found in most American Indian music east of the Mississippi River.

CONCLUSIONS

Our conclusions about rhythm in primitive music must be general. We find a great variety of phenomena and none that contrast essentially with Western music. The lack of theory and established terminology for describing rhythmic phenomena necessitates our rather sketchy characterization. We are sure of one fact: that rhythmic complexity correlates in most primitive styles with the general level of sophistication of the music. Our discussion of form leads us to conclude that unifying factors are intrinsic, and that the most widespread one is some sort of repetition. Simple repetition or variation of a short phrase is the basis of the litany-type form; it is also found in strophic materials, where the use of transposition is also important. Repetition and variation of very short motifs which are hard to identify are present in through-composed forms also. Reverting and iterative elements occur more frequently than purely progressive ones. We have found that formal complexity can be measured to some extent by the number of elements involved and by the number of their interrelationships, and that complex forms usually accompany complex melodic organization but not as frequently complex rhythmic structure.

Polyphony

Primitive music with more than one melodic part has attracted a disproportionate amount of attention from scholars, although as yet not all the styles and ramifications of it are known. This type of music comprises a relatively small part of the primitive repertory. The great majority of music in preliterate cultures is monophonic, and even in most areas where polyphony is known and well developed, most songs are still monophonic.

DEFINITION OF PRIMITIVE POLYPHONY

In Western European music theory it is customary to differentiate between polyphony and homophony: in polyphonic music the voices are independent (in some sense, although they obviously must have certain interrelationships in each style), whereas in homophonic music one voice stands out and dominates the others. In primitive music such a distinction cannot readily be made. It is difficult to ascertain, from statements of native informants, whether certain kinds of part relationships are homophonic or polyphonic in the Western sense. If questioned about the relative importance of voices, most natives do not respond well. And little can be said by the outsider; chordal structures and chord "feelings" are rarely detected in primitive music by Western listeners. Thus we cannot, except in such obvious cases as the drone or the ostinato types of part music, assign to one voice primacy over the others. In consequence we designate all music polyphonic in which we hear more than one pitch simultaneously. The distinction between this definition and the Western concept of the term should be carefully noted. There is one exception: singing in octaves is found wherever men and women sing together in primitive groups, and it is ordinarily considered not polyphony but rather a special type of monophonic performance that is modified by the physiological limits of the human voice.

THEORIES ON ORIGIN

Polyphony is found in all corners of the world. Its similarity to various Western European styles cannot, in the vast majority of cases, be ascribed to European influence, nor can remote historical connections with Europe be postulated in most instances. The origin of polyphony has been the subject of many debates and literary discussions. Among the earliest explanations is the theory of fusibility, the result of an experiment in the psychology of music by H. L. F. Helmholtz, the eminent acoustician.[1] The gist of Helmholtz' theory is that the simpler the mathematical ratio of an interval, the more difficult it is for the human ear to distinguish between the tones of the interval. A great many people can not distinguish between tones an octave apart; the ratio of an octave is the simplest, 2:1. The number of people who can not differentiate the tones of a perfect fifth, whose ratio is 2:3, is somewhat smaller; fewer still can not distinguish the perfect fourth, whose ratio is 3:4; and so on for the thirds and seconds. Consequently, Helmholtz believed that polyphony probably originated when some individuals incapable of discrimination began singing in perfect fifths, and others, recognizing and appreciating the sound for what it was, imitated it and initiated a tradition.

Although the theory of fusibility as such has been validated through experiments, the conclusions concerning polyphony that are based on this theory are probably not justified. In some parts of the world, polyphony may have developed according to Helmholtz' description; such development has been postulated for those cultures using parallel fifths and other kinds of parallel intervals. But it does not explain the origin of other types of polyphony.

The theory of latent harmony has been discussed on page 33. Fillmore's assumption that some feeling for harmony exists in all primitive musicians has been widely adopted, but it is completely unsubstantiated. Rather than describing the primitive material objectively or from the point of view of native participants, the researcher who accepts the concept of latent harmony only gives the reactions to primitive music of a person steeped in Western musical concepts, plus his attempts to adjust the primitive material to his own musical environment. The assumption that polyphony is bound to spring up automatically in every musical style as soon as the performers have become sufficiently sophisticated to be aware of the harmonic implications of their monophonic music does not hold water. For one thing, the presence of polyphony does not necessarily presuppose complexity in other aspects of music. In African Negro music, where polyphony is probably more complex than anywhere else, the development of melody is at a simple level. In most North American Indian music, where melody is complex, polyphony is not found. In Micronesia, where one of the simplest of all styles prevails, polyphony is present. The tone systems of polyphonic materials in a given style do not often coincide with the tone systems of the individual parts; this discrepancy is strong evidence against the beginnings of polyphony from a feeling of latent harmony. Furthermore, those primitive styles in which prevail large intervals and triad-like progressions, the bases of the Western concept of latent harmony, are by no means more likely to use polyphony than are those styles in which small intervals, the traditional material for "pure" melody, dominate.

Marius Schneider's book on polyphony, *Geschichte der Mehrstimmigkeit*, shows the influence of the German *Kulturkreis*, or evolution-of-culture, school of anthropology. In this survey, the majority of the primitive styles using polyphony have been classified under four "areas" that correspond to the *Kulturkreis* concept — they are noncontiguous and supposedly delimit historical periods as well as geographic cultural boundaries. The areas were determined on the basis of two main criteria: the similarity or diversity between the tonal organization of the individual parts;

and the equality or inequality of the importance of the individual parts. The first area, which is distributed throughout the world, has only the polyphonic form called "variant-heterophony." This means that the voices by and large perform the same material but that occasional errors or deviations by single performers create some polyphonic segments. The accidental lapsing into parallel fifths, fourths, etc., by singers is included in this area. All the voices are of equal importance and all use the same tonal organization. This area includes the simplest musical styles, most of which have no actual polyphony, in our sense of the word, in a consistent way. Schneider's second area includes Southeast Asia, Melanesia, and Micronesia. It is characterized by various forms of polyphony, such as drones, parallel intervals, and canons, in which each voice has a separate tonal organization. The third area, which comprises Samoa and some other parts of Polynesia, is distinguished from the second by more varied relationships between them. The fourth area, Africa, has even more forms of polyphony; its outstanding characteristic is a tendency towards homophony.

Schneider believes that each area is at a stage of musical development through which all areas pass at some time, the view taken by the *Kulturkreis* school. His definition of tonal organization is essentially that of Western theory, with special accommodations for pentatonic materials. His emphasis differs from that of most ethnomusicologists: he pays more attention to tonal organization and to the relative importance of individual parts than to the type of relationship between them. Because the aspects Schneider emphasizes depend partly on the intuitive feelings of the investigator and partly on verbalization by native informants, we believe it preferable in this book to try to classify the types of polyphony according to the relationships between the parts, and then to outline their distribution.

HETEROPHONY

Most polyphonic music employs identical or similar materials in each part. This statement applies, of course, to the three most common forms of polyphony: heterophony, parallel intervals, and imitation. Heterophony, the use of slightly modified versions of the same melody by two or more performers, is the simplest in some ways, because it can come about accidentally, e.g., a solo performer may vary his part slightly while singing essentially unison material with a group. While heterophony is found in most areas of the world, it is not a conspicuous facet of primitive polyphony. Probably most of the primitive examples of it that we have were accidental phenomena. Rhythmic variation is very likely the commonest form. It is shown in Example 37, a song for voice and musical bow from Equatorial Africa. The two carry the same melody, but the voice uses three durational values while the bow performs with only one.

Although heterophony is not strong in primitive music, it is the main type of polyphony in Oriental cultivated music, where it assumes very complex forms. Thus heterophony is not necessarily simple and accidental; it may be elaborate and detailed. Its absence in primitive cultures may indicate that it is not of primordial origin and that it has not been the starting point for the development of other types of polyphony.

PARALLEL INTERVALS

Part music performed in parallel intervals is probably the most common type of polyphony in the world. Various intervals are used, and the degree of restriction to complete parallelism differs. Singing in parallel octaves has been mentioned as being almost universal and thus not acceptable as true polyphony. We find the parallel fifth, the most commonly used interval, in a number of places throughout the world, including many parts of Negro Africa (particularly the eastern section), some parts of the Caucasus and central Asia, and, in the realm of folk music, in Iceland. The structure is not usually consistently parallel, but fairly close to being so. In Example 38 of the Shona Karanga of northern Rhodesia, only a part of the material is in parallel fifths; there is some overlapping, and there are also monophonic sections in which one part or another is resting.

A passage that sounds peculiarly like some of the organum of the early Middle Ages is found in Example 39 from the Tonga of northern Rhodesia. A three-part chorus of boys and an alternating solo singer are accompanied by a musical bow that also plays introductory, interpolated, and terminal solo material. The choral singers sing only in parallel fourths and fifths, the highest part being removed from the lowest by an octave. The range of the musical bow is restricted, so that it cannot follow the entire melodic line of any single choral part. Consequently it begins playing in unison with the middle part and, when the voices ascend, it changes to the lowest part. In this case we see strict singing in parallel intervals modified by the alternation of the musical bow between two parts. Each part has a separate tonal organization, since the strict parallelism includes no diminished fifths or augmented fourths that betray the adjustment of one part to the tonal organization of another.

A variety of singing in parallel fifths that is so complex it could also be classified as independent part music is found among some tribes in the Caucasus and in central Asia near the Caspian Sea. These forms are surprisingly similar to certain types of medieval European cultivated music. They resemble some kinds of organum, some of the works of Machaut, and, in a few cases, sixteenth-century styles. Of course they could not actually be mistaken for their European counterparts, but the resemblance is of great interest and has been noted by many scholars, including Schneider, Lach, and Victor Belayev.[2] Example 40 from the Gur, on the shores of the Caspian Sea, is characteristic. The framework of parallel fifths, the suspensions, and a type of movement in the lowest voice that is akin to European root movement make this example stand out as especially similar to European materials.

The origin of this type has often been discussed. While it has been accepted that the use of parallel fifths as such has multiple origins, one of which according to the theory of fusibility may be the simple acoustic ratio of the fifth, material so specialized and still so similar to European polyphony has been thought to be historically connected with organum. Belayev believes that this type of polyphony had a wider distribution in the folk music of the Middle Ages than it has today, and that it was accepted by the cultivated musicians of medieval Europe in ready-made form. The presence of parallel fifths in Iceland substantiates this theory, since it suggests that the type was at one time present everywhere between these widely separated points, and that it was subsequently replaced by other types in the center of the area (Europe) while remaining unchanged on the periphery.

Gustave Reese believes that European organum and the similar Caucasian parallel form sprang up independently.[3] Since the two types are so similar and yet each is so complex, Reese's theory is hard to accept. The likelihood of European influence in the Caucasus also seems far-fetched, although it should be considered in the case of Iceland. It is unlikely that the tribes in the Caucasus and central Asia had direct contact with European cultivated music, because if they had been influenced by the music of any high culture it would probably have been that of the Arabic-Persian groups, with whom they were in close contact, and these groups had practically no parallel fifths or polyphony in general. Thus the problem remains unsolved. One possibility is a connection with polyphonic Russian folk music, which is somewhat different from the types discussed here but which may have been related to European cultivated music originally. It is possible that the Caucasian polyphonic forms evolved from material that was primarily in parallel fifths but adapted according to Russian folk models. If such is the case, the fact that the Caucasian songs resemble medieval polyphony is purely coincidental. Since we have, as usual, no historical records of the early developments of the Caucasian polyphonic music and since we do not know how far back it goes, this assumption is reasonable.

Parallel fifths and fourths are found in about the same distribution, a fact which seems to lend validity to the theory of the invertability of intervals and the theory of fusibility, since it illustrates inability to differentiate tones an octave apart. Parallel fourths occur somewhat less frequently than fifths; they are relatively common in east Africa and rather rare in the Caucasus and central Asia. Parallel thirds are found in many areas. In

European music theory, "parallel" in reference to thirds implies the use of both major and minor thirds alternating in various combinations. In primitive music as well as European, parallel heterogeneous thirds are common, while strict parallelism of only major or only minor thirds is rare. In most styles that use parallel thirds, they are heterogeneous. Such styles are heavily concentrated in Melanesia, Micronesia, and Negro Africa, particularly West Africa, where there may be a connection with the predominance of thirds as melodic intervals. Major thirds predominate in Africa, while in the South Seas minor thirds are more frequent. This distribution may be based on the size of range in these styles: in West Africa relatively large ranges are the rule, while in Micronesia they are rarely more than a fifth. Example 41 from Micronesia is illustrative of predominating minor thirds. In Example 42 from the Belgian Congo, parallel thirds are combined with the characteristic African responsorial form. In this example, thirds also appear out of parallel construction, but no other intervals are used at all.

Parallel seconds are not only present in primitive music but are relatively widespread. Major seconds predominate, although heterogeneous ones are found in some styles. Parallel seconds are always associated with small ranges. They are found in Micronesia, in some parts of northeast Africa (not ordinarily among Negro groups, however), and in the folk music of the Balkans. The Lombards, a barbarian tribe that settled in northern Italy, are known to have "howled" in seconds, we find from Renaissance records.[4] Example 43, from the Caroline Islands, illustrates strict parallelism in seconds.

Finally, we should mention some less common intervals used as the basis for parallel motion. These may, in some cases, be accidental. At any rate, they are not widely distributed or of great strength in those styles where they occur. One recording of California Indian (Miwok) songs includes singing in parallel major thirds. The author has also been told that the Salish Indians of Washington sing in augmented fourths, which the informant observed during each of three annual trips to the same settlement. In this instance the polyphony may not have been accidental but rather the invention of individual musicians in the culture, the type of deviation that does not take root among the populace as a whole but becomes general practice in isolated communities. Whether the practice will eventually become the property of the entire culture cannot be ascertained. Western music abounds in inventions of musical styles and in stylistic elements that have been confined to a small group of participants and never accepted by the culture as a whole, and the same situation may well exist in primitive cultures.

IMITATION

The third type of primitive polyphony is imitation, which includes close imitation, canons and rounds, and briefly overlapping parts. Some scholars have conjectured that overlapping was the original type of imitation, from which the others developed. The theory is strengthened by the fact that imitation coincides with antiphonal and responsorial techniques in many styles, specifically in Polynesia, Malaya, the eastern part of North America, and most strongly of course in Negro Africa. It seems likely that responsorial techniques were the basis for overlapping, the simplest form of imitation. In some cases we have been able to observe the development of overlapping from monophonic passages. Let us consider a hypothetical situation in which a leader and a chorus are alternately repeating the same phrase. The members of our imaginary chorus, who know their parts well and are somewhat impatient to enter, begin to sing their phrase before the leader has completed his; the result would be a very simple canon, even though the voices would overlap only on one or two notes. Example 44 is the opening of an Arapaho song that may have grown by such a process: the leader begins, and his phrase is interrupted and repeated by the group before both join in the completion of the song. Here the imitation is at the simplest possible level and not truly polyphonic, as there is an interval of only a fifth between the parts at the point of overlap. Nevertheless, it demonstrates the spontaneous beginning of imitative polyphony. We still must question whether impatience of repeating voices in antiphonal songs is responsible for all imitation; it certainly accounts for some cases but probably not for all.

Strict canons in the Western sense occur infrequently. The form in primitive music is usually combined with other types of polyphonic movement. For example, the parts of a song may begin in canonic structure, and then one part may move in a free melodic line while the other becomes an ostinato accompaniment. Example 35 from equatorial Africa and Example 45 from Malaka are typical of songs with a canonic beginning. In songs from the island of Flores in Indonesia, the canon is sung over a drone of a perfect fifth, a form that resembles certain European canons like the famous "Sumer is icumen in." No historical connection between the two has been conjectured as yet.

The musical items containing canons are usually long. The harmonic intervals in canons are likely to conform with the Western concepts of consonance and dissonance, since in most cases "consonant" intervals fall on a point of rhythmic stress. Indeed, fifths, fourths, thirds, and sixths are more prevalent than seconds and sevenths in primitive canons. This information is of purely descriptive value, for there are no known rules of consonance and dissonance operating in primitive music that are comparable to the strict European ones. It is difficult to formulate any harmonic laws from what we know of primitive polyphony; we can determine which intervals tend to coincide with stressed beats and which do not, but in no style have intervals been classified according to their rhythmic positions.

OTHER TYPES OF POLYPHONY

A slightly less common type, although a somewhat simpler one, is the combination of a drone, or bourdon, with a moving melody. This type, found in Polynesia and southwest Asia, is strongly represented in Negro Africa and in a few songs of the North Pacific Coast of North America. It occurs in two main forms: a steady drone and an interrupted drone consisting of a number of repetitions of the same pitch. Example 46, from the Futuna Islands in Polynesia, is typical of an interrupted drone, which is the main polyphonic form of that area. The lower voice repeats one pitch while the upper moves with more freedom. An interesting form of the interrupted drone is found in the Peyote songs. A monophonic melody is accompanied by a drum. The drum, which is tuned by moistening the drumhead, is expected to stay at a certain pitch that usually duplicates one of the important melodic tones. The principle is similar to that of the Western kettledrum. The interval between the drone and the tonic of the melody is usually an octave or a perfect fifth or fourth.

A related type of correspondence between the parts of a polyphonic piece is the ostinato: a short section is repeated a number of times, while another more progressive part is sung. The ostinato may have developed from the interrupted drone, since the latter, a single repeated tone, could gradually become a succession of two repeated tones and finally a more elaborate repeated phrase. The ostinato patterns are always very short in primitive music, shorter than, for example, the sixteenth-century basses in Western cultivated music. In Example 47 from equatorial Africa, the ostinato pattern of the sansas (finger xylophones), which accompany the longer melodic unit of the soloist, is an extension of antiphonal technique.

In the more complex African styles, both the drone or ostinato and the melody are found in polyphonic form. In Example 48 from the Shona Karanga, a group of sansas carry the ostinato, within which several parts are relatively independent. The individual ostinato sections are varied in the usual African Negro manner. The melody, sung by a group of men, is antiphonal and litany-type in form. Considering this as typical, we may say that ostinato specimens of primitive music are dissimilar to those of Western cultivated music: the melodic part in the latter is likely to be progressive, relatively nonrepetitive, while in primitive music it is usually of the litany-type form.

Somewhat related to this combination of ostinato and independent melodic parts is a type common in African music but not elsewhere, consisting of a repetitive section in each part with little regulated relationship among the parts. Each of the relatively independent parts is of the simple litany-type form. This type has the greatest degree of independence of parts as yet found in primitive music to any large extent. One of the simplest examples is the polyphony produced by a single musical bow (see the description on p. 101). Here the player, besides producing contrast in pitch by plucking the string, uses his open mouth as a resonator. If he changes the aperture of his mouth, he is able to produce various audible overtones. So two sets of tones are heard: the fundamentals produced by plucking the string and the overtones. The relationship between a fundamental and its overtone is not evidently subject to any laws within the style. An independent relationship among the various parts is more common in instrumental polyphony than in vocal; perhaps because the limits of the technique of the instrument govern the style and in consequence other unifying factors are less necessary. Example 49 is played on the musical bow alone, without the usual accompaniment of the human voice.

CONCLUSIONS

Our discussion of primitive polyphony has identified two basic kinds of relationship between the various parts: (1) equality of parts in importance, usually accompanied by the presence of the same musical material in all the parts, and (2) hierarchy of parts, which occurs in songs containing a drone or an ostinato, and where the less important parts always include less material than the main ones. In the latter case, the whole piece is usually governed by litany-type form. The vast majority of primitive polyphonic pieces are in two parts; some are in three or four, but these are much rarer.

Few generalizations can be made about harmonic intervals in primitive music. The best estimate possible is that there are no rules followed closely, as are those in European cultivated music concerning the position and order or harmonic intervals.

The styles using the most complex polyphony are found in Negro Africa and western Asia. Some polyphony is present in Polynesia, Micronesia, Indonesia, and Malaya, as well as southern India. Small, rudimentary forms of polyphony are found in some parts of South America (notably Patagonia), the Northwest Coast of North America, the eastern United States, and to a lesser degree, the Great Plains. On the whole, no polyphony has been found in the main portion of the New World and in Northern and Eastern Asia. The presence of polyphony seems to coincide with the presence of elaborate melodic instruments; much extant polyphonic music is instrumental. However, polyphony does not indicate a necessarily complex style in other aspects of music, and even in those areas where polyphony is strongly developed the majority of the songs are monophonic.

Musical instruments

The study of musical instruments in primitive cultures is closely allied with the study of musical instruments in high cultures, since similar forms are often found in both. Instruments have been spreading throughout the world for centuries. We can trace some of their movements archeologically, and we have observed their wanderings over entire continents and across oceans within the last few centuries. The study of instruments is important for the ethnologist interested in material culture; in some primitive societies instruments constitute a substantial proportion of the objects made by the craftsmen, and often they are the most complex products of human workmanship in a culture. Because of their diffusion, instruments are also of great importance to the historian of culture. They are usually relatively complex and thus are not likely to have been invented more than once. The presence of the same instrumental form in widely separated areas, therefore, indicates some relationship between these areas and allows us to assume some previous contact between their inhabitants. The study of instruments is the aspect of ethnomusicology that ties it to archeology; very little can be learned of prehistoric musical styles and practices except what is gleaned from the instruments found in archeological sites.

CLASSIFICATIONS OF INSTRUMENTS

The instruments of the world are found in many different forms. Indeed, Curt Sachs's dictionary of instruments, *Real-Lexikon der Musikinstrumente*, includes more than ten thousand separate entries of instrumental forms and does not pretend to be complete. Of course, many of these individual forms are interrelated and stem from the same ancestor. Thus some kind of classification is a useful educational device. As Sachs and Hornbostel, the authors of the most important classification, readily admit, classifications cannot take account of the historical movements of the instruments.[1] They do not help in interpreting their history because the descendants of one instrument may be in a different class from the parent, depending on the method of classification used. The value of classifying instruments, then, lies in helping the student identify an instrument form and compare it with similar ones, in making it possible for a museum curator to place similar instruments together, and in giving a means whereby an instrument may be readily identified by a single word instead of by a description of all its characteristics.

There are three main methods of classification: (1) according to material culture, (2) according to musical style, and (3) according to the acoustic principles involved in sound production. Classification according to material culture generally uses the materials of which instruments are made as the main criteria. Such was the classification scheme of the ancient Chinese, who recognized five classes — wood, metal, etc.[2] Classification according to musical style is used in the conventional division of symphony orchestras into string, wood-wind, brass, and percussion sections. The brass instruments have certain stylistic functions, the strings others, and so on. Classification of a modern orchestra by the first method would result in quite different groupings, since flutes are generally made of metal, clarinets and violins of wood, and so on. Classification by structural material agrees neither with classification by style nor with that by acoustic principles, although there are occasional resemblances. Stylistic classification is not particularly useful for a cross-cultural and cross-stylistic treatment, since one instrument may serve different stylistic functions in the music of different cultures and may be allied with various forms.

Classification according to acoustic principles is the method considered most useful by specialists in musical instruments. This classification, although approached by Mahillon[3] in the nineteenth century, is primarily the work of Curt Sachs, the man to whom students of musical instruments are also indebted for enormous compilations of comparative data and for far-reaching theories on origin and development. It is important to keep in mind that all of Sachs's schemes for the classification and distribution of instruments include not only primitive but also folk and cultivated ones. The system of classification according to acoustic principles that he and Hornbostel presented in an article in 1914 [4] includes four main classes: (1) idiophones, instruments whose bodies vibrate to produce the sound, (2) aerophones, instruments that enclose a column of air which vibrates, (3) membranophones, instruments that have a vibrating membrane, and (4) chordophones, those with vibrating strings. A few isolated types cannot be classified according to this method, but the vast majority of instruments easily find a place in the scheme.

The idiophone is probably the most common type of instrument throughout the world. It includes rattles, various kinds of percussion instruments without vibrating membranes, xylophones and bells, and many others. They appear in both simple and complex forms. For example, a bell or rattle vibrates in its entirety and thus is a simple idiophone; a xylophone, in which each key vibrates separately, is a complex idiophone, each key being a simple one in itself. Sachs distinguishes further between idiophones that are struck directly by the player, such as bells and log drums, and those like rattles, where the striking is caused by another type of motion, such as swinging or shaking. Plucked and strummed idiophones are also found, but rarely.

Aerophones include all those that are popularly called wind instruments. Again we find simple and complex forms, the trumpets, clarinets, and flutes being simple and the panpipes, organs, and other multiple-tube instruments being complex. Sachs distinguishes between trumpet-type, flute-type, and reed instruments. The trumpet-type ones, which are identified by the fact that the lips of the performer vibrate and cause the column of air to vibrate, are divided into trumpets, whose bore is cylindrical, and horns, whose bore is conical. In flute-type instruments, a ribbon-shaped column of air is produced and directed against a sharp edge, causing it to vacillate and thus set the large column of air inside the instrument vibrating. These are divided into true flutes and whistle-flutes or recorders. In true flutes the ribbon-shaped column of air is produced between the lips and directed against the edge of the aperture. In recorders this column of air is produced between a plug in the mouthpiece and the flute wall and is directed against the edge of another hole further down the body of the instrument. Reed instruments also operate this way, with the column of air produced between the two parts of a double reed, as in the oboe, or between the reed and the mouthpiece, as in the clarinet. Multiple tubes and the presence or absence of finger holes are further means of classification.

Membranophones include instruments with one or two drum-heads and with various shapes. This type is the simplest and least diversified of the four. Membranophones are, however, very widespread. It should be pointed out that not all of the instruments usually called drums are true membranophones. Those which have no skin head, such as the so-called log drums, are idiophones.

Chordophones are probably the least widespread of the four types of instruments. They are found in many different forms and are classified according to the number of strings, the presence or absence of a bow, and the manner of playing: plucking, striking, bowing, rubbing, etc. The presence of frets and the shape of the body are also factors.

THEORIES OF INSTRUMENT DISTRIBUTION

In analyzing the geographic distribution of instruments, we are able to apply the two important methods of anthropological area study that we have mentioned before: the *Kulturkreis* approach and the American culture area approach. The point of view of the *Kulturkreis* school has been ably set forth by Sachs in his book *Geist und Werden der Musikinstrumente*. Sachs has mapped out the distribution of instruments, analyzed it according to the culture circles of Gräbner, Schmidt, Ankermann, Preuss, and others, and has discovered that they correlate. Since

the circles indicate historical periods, Sachs's classification led
to some interesting discoveries. He finds, for example, that certain very simple instruments — such as rattles, scrapers, and the
slapping of various parts of the human body — have almost
world-wide distribution and thus may be the oldest instruments
common to all men. Certain geographic areas, not always contiguous and sometimes separated by oceans, were characterized
by individual instruments and instrumental types and could
thus be assigned their position both in geography and history.
As is usual in the *Kulturkreis* schemes, the areas overlapped; a
particular geographic location might be part of more than one
culture circle.

More recently, Sachs has modified his earlier *Kulturkreis* approach to one that uses three main categories or periods.[5] These
periods coincide with geographic distributions. Instruments that
have world-wide distribution, like rattles, are the oldest. Others
that have a smaller distribution but are nevertheless found in
diverse culture areas and continents — the xylophone, the musical bow, and the true flute — are next in age. The most recent
are those confined to one culture area, such as the sansa of Negro
Africa and the pianoforte of western Europe. This scheme is
plausible, although there may be exceptions to it. Sachs's earlier
scheme did not always give complete distributions of instruments
(at the time of publication of his book, in 1929, they may not
have been known), and consequently it may have important gaps.
Furthermore, most American anthropologists would probably take
exception to the *Kulturkreis* theoretical approach.

In order to discuss the distribution of musical instruments
according to the American culture area approach, that concept
must be briefly explained.[6] A "culture area" is a locale whose inhabitants share a relatively homogeneous culture. For example,
since the Eskimos all have kayaks, a knowledge of sewing, sea
mammals as the staple food, similar bodies of mythology, and
ice houses, they are considered as inhabiting one culture area.
The Negroes of East Africa are all members of one culture area,
called the Eastern Cattle area: they all have domesticated cattle,
patrilineal descent, age-grade societies, and round-shaped houses.

Western Europe is another culture area; its inhabitants all use a certain type of clothing, share in monotheistic religions, have knowledge of the wheel and many technological devices based on it, and also have patrilineal descent. The centers of culture areas can be demarcated quite clearly, but the boundaries are not exact; they are inhabited by peoples who share the cultural traits of all the adjoining areas. The culture area is not assumed to be necessarily a historical unit. It is primarily of classificatory value.

The distribution of musical instruments often correlates with other cultural traits and helps in the identification of culture areas. In fact, the distribution of musical instruments is usually more closely related to culture areas in general than are musical styles. For example, the use of bird whistles in North America is confined by and large to the Northwest Coast culture area. On the other hand, many types of musical instruments are found in more than one culture area and may be characteristic of entire continents or even hemispheres.

CASE STUDIES

The available information on world-wide instrumental distribution is far from exhaustive; only a sampling has been made. Even so, large books have not been able to cover the facts already known, for the detailed study of this field would be a lifelong task for more than a few scholars. We shall only attempt here a brief survey of the instruments used by the Indians of North and South America and by the African Negroes, and we shall follow this by examining briefly certain primitive instruments of special interest.

American Indians. The North American Indians have relatively few instruments, and most of those are nonmelodic. Most tribes have tambourine drums, except those in the extreme South of the continent. In the southwestern and southeastern United States the water drum is widely used. This instrument has one head that is stretched over a ceramic pot, which has been partly filled with water in order to tune it and achieve the desirable tone. All the American Indians beat their drums with sticks.

The most widely used instrument type in North America is the idiophone. Rattles are the most numerous form, being the property of practically every tribe. Container rattles are made of rawhide in the North and gourds in the South and enclose a number of pebbles. Deerhoof rattles consist of about twenty doe hooves suspended from a stick. They are used throughout the continent as well as in South America and seem to be frequently used in puberty rites for girls, according to Harold Driver and S. H. Riesenberg.[7] Turtle-shell rattles are also common in a number of areas. Another type, the notched-stick idiophone, consists of a stick in which notches have been cut, over which a second stick is rubbed to make a rasping sound. It is found largely in the western part of the United States, especially in the Great Basin of Nevada and Utah, where some tribes have no other instruments at all.[8] Simpler idiophones, those struck directly by the player, are used less often than rattles. They are concentrated most heavily along the North Pacific Coast.[9] The most common form is a plank which is beaten, although a number of other idiophones are found with narrower distributions.

The simplest aerophones, which are very widely distributed throughout the continent but used primarily as toys, are the "bullroarer," a small hard object swung in the air from a string, and the "bonebuzzer," a piece of bone revolving rapidly and controlled by two strings. Whistles made of wood and of bird bones, without finger holes, are widespread. Both true flutes and recorders are found everywhere except in parts of the Great Basin. They have from four to six finger holes and are tuned in intervals usually ranging between a major second and a minor third. The most complex development of the aerophone is found on the North Pacific Coast,[10] where besides the usual flutes and straight whistles we find wooden whistles carved in the shapes of birds. There are also multiple whistles: two or three whistles are strapped together, on which are played shrill, harsh-sounding chords to accompany certain ceremonies. They are not used for melodic material.

There have been reports that the musical bow exists in California and a few other places in the southwestern United States,[11] but the information comes from people who had only heard about the bow and apparently hardly ever saw one. To my knowledge, its music has never been recorded.

In Mexico, where Indian culture tends to be more sophisticated than in the United States, practically all the same instrument forms occur developed to a higher degree of complexity. Log drums (*teponatzli*) and conch-shell trumpets have been discovered. The presence of bird-shaped whistles is evidence of a cultural relationship to the North Pacific Coast Indians. The Mexican notched sticks are elaborately carved in animal forms, with hollow bodies that serve as resonators. Reed instruments are also in use. Again, the musical bow is probably not used to any great extent.[12]

There is as yet no definitive book on North American instruments. However, Karl Gustav Izikowitz has made an intensive study of those in South America, using both enthnological and archeological sources.[13] He has not given the complete distribution of every instrument, a gigantic task that will probably never be completed since there are many hundreds of tribes; but he has given a representative picture of every important type and form. The South American instruments resemble the North American in many ways, although there are many more types and forms. Some of the instruments not found in North America are panpipes, bells made of metal and other substances, fruit-shell rattles, simple reed aerophones and trumpet-type instruments, two-headed drums, stamping tubes, and musical bows, which are definitely present in Patagonia. It is possible that some instruments, particularly the stamping tubes and a xylophone found only among the Witoto of northern Brazil, were imported by Negroes from Africa. The greater complexity of South American instruments may be traced, among other factors, to the wealth of natural materials, to possible contact with tribes of other continents, and to the existence of literate societies like that of the Incas, who deliberately influenced other cultures.

From this outline of instruments in the Americas, we can see that they are likely to be complex and abundant in the generally complex cultures, especially those with material wealth. How-

ever, advanced instrumental development does not necessarily
imply complexity of musical style. Throughout the Americas, the
role of instrumental music is small compared to that of vocal
music, although tribesmen sometimes consider particular instruments to be of great importance because they have symbolic
significance. Furthermore, even though compared to other primitive groups the American tribes have not developed far instru-
mentally, their instruments are surprisingly numerous and varied,
with real paucity occurring only in parts of the Great Basin.

African Negroes. The instruments of the African Negroes are
very complex and occur in so many forms that only a small number of them can be mentioned or described here. The area of
greatest complexity is West Africa; south of the Congo instruments are somewhat simpler. Instrumental solos are rather rare
in Africa. The ensembles may consist of one type of instrument
or may combine several, and frequently are used in conjunction
with solo and choral singing.

All of the four acoustic classes are amply represented. Among
the simple idiophones we find, of course, various kinds of rattles,
including those made of basketry, bells, and clappers, and log
drums that are often used for signaling. The Africans, as we have
seen, possess the xylophone, which is today considered a typical
African instrument despite its probable origin in Indonesia. The
simplest xylophones have only one key, a single slab of wood.
Others consist of a few unattached slabs that are put across two
small tree trunks for playing. More complex ones have the slabs
fastened to cross-pieces and include calabash resonators and a
contrivance for suspending the instrument from the player's
neck. They are often played in groups, although in some areas
a single large xylophone is played by two or three performers at
once.[14]

An instrument peculiar to Negro Africa is the sansa, also
called the finger-xylophone or thumb piano, which evidently
developed from the xylophone. It consists of a number of tongues
of either metal or reed that are attached to cross-pieces and
mounted on a board or box so that the tongues protrude. Sometimes an additional resonator is attached. Each tongue is a simple

idiophone, making the entire instrument a complex one. It takes up no more than six square inches of space altogether. The number of tongues varies from eight to thirty-six, the average being about fifteen.[15] The protruding ends of the tongues are stroked by the player to produce a very soft sound similar to that of a xylophone but with more of a plucked quality. Sansas are used both in ensembles and as an accompaniment for singers.

Membranophones in Africa are played often in groups of three, sometimes of only two. They occupy positions of prominence in the cultures and may be venerated and given individual names. Sex symbolism is frequently involved. The performers are usually men,[16] who beat on the drums with sticks, fingers, or knuckles. The techniques of performance and the rhythmic style are very elaborate. Contrasting pitches in the ensemble are essential, as is true also with groups of idiophones.

Aerophones of various kinds include bullroarers and buzzing disks, plus instruments of the flute, trumpet, and reed types, both simple and complex. An interesting development has taken place among Bushmen and Hottentot flutists. It is known as hocket technique because of its similarity to a technique used in medieval polyphony that has the same name. Each of a number of players has a flute capable of producing only one pitch (except by overblowing, which is never done deliberately). A melody is played by each musician's chiming in with his tone at the proper time and resting otherwise. Even polyphony has been performed by hocket technique. Panpipes may have developed from this method (or perhaps it was the other way around), since they are also found in Africa. Hocket technique, which is evidently very old, is used in ensembles of reed flutes as well; Vasco da Gama observed them as early as 1497.[17] Other aerophones of particular interest are horns made of ivory and wood, which are often used for signaling and are owned by royalty and chiefs. Some of the horns have finger-holes and are played very rapidly. Antelope horns are also used as musical instruments; in some cases they are as long as five feet.

Chordophones are plentiful in Negro Africa. Of greatest interest is the musical bow, which is widely used in many forms. In

South Africa it is practically the only chordophone; farther
north and along the West Coast there are many more complex
ones. The musical bow is made of a single string that is attached
to and stretched by a bent piece of wood like a hunting bow. The
bow, which is sometimes notched, consists of a flat piece of wood
or a hollow reed; the string is of plant fiber or rawhide.[18] A tone
is produced by plucking the string or striking or rubbing it with
a stick. Today the instrument often has a resonator attached,
such as a calabash or a tin can. The mouth is also used as a
resonator, as we have seen. Occasionally two bows are played
simultaneously. The instrument is evidently of ancient derivation, as it has been depicted in rock paintings. Most other stringed
instruments in Africa resemble Oriental forms or the plucked
instruments of Eurasia, such as the guitar. They usually have
few strings. Harps have been found in the West and Northeast;
they are often made of palm fiber and have approximately six
strings, and their primary function is accompanying singers.

The xylophone. Some instruments used in primitive cultures
are of special interest, either because of their distribution, or
because they are unique to primitive peoples, or possibly because
they have helped anthropologists and historians of culture to
validate certain theories. The xylophone commands attention
because of its history. It evidently originated in southeast Asia,
and it has spread almost entirely around the world. Approximately fifteen hundred years ago, a group of Malayo-Polynesian
speaking peoples migrated to Africa, probably to Madagascar,
and carried it with them. This fact has been generally accepted,
since certain tribes in Madagascar speak Malayo-Polynesian languages and since Kunst has found some correspondences in the
tuning of Indonesian and African xylophones.[19] The highest
development of the xylophone is in the area nearest Madagascar,
and further evidence for its importation lies in the similarity of
the East African xylophone orchestras to the gamelan orchestras
of Java and Bali. From Africa the xylophone traveled to the New
World via Negro slaves. It was adopted by European symphony
orchestras and also by some Central and South American Indian
tribes, where it has become so ingrained that some of the natives

consider it indigenous. The sansa is perhaps a special African development of the xylophone, possibly originated under the influence of the prevalent plucked-string technique of African chordophones. It is not found outside Negro Africa except among certain Negro groups in the New World.

Panpipes. Panpipes are of considerable interest because of their wide geographic distribution. The ancient Greeks knew them by the name of syrinx. Today they exist in practically all parts of the eastern hemisphere, particularly southeast Asia, Melanesia, Polynesia,[20] and Africa. They are also used in the western part of South America, where their presence is something of a puzzle. They have played a fairly important role in the controversies about the possibility of contact between the Polynesians and the South American Indians. Most scholars have not considered the mere presence of panpipes in both areas sufficient evidence for assuming contact, because the structure of panpipes is so simple that independent inventions are conceivable.[21] However, the fact that tuning of the pipes is identical in both places has fostered the theory that the culture moved from Polynesia to South America. Again, this evidence is not conclusive, for the pipes are tuned in perfect fourths, an interval so acoustically simple that its duplication might be accidental. Although this problem remains unsolved, it illustrates how a musical instrument may figure in attempts to determine cultural movements.

The musical bow. The simplest type of musical bow is probably the so-called "earth-bow," a string stretched across a hole in the ground, which functions as a resonator. Musical bows of the conventional structure described on page 88 are widespread throughout the world; they have been found in many parts of the Old World and in Patagonia, and may have existed in California and ancient Mexico. Because of its wide distribution, Sachs has formulated the theory that the musical bow is the ancestor of all stringed instruments.[22] This is debatable because the musical bow closely resembles the hunting bow, which was evidently invented in Europe during the Mesolithic period and thence spread throughout the earth. We know that the hunting

bow has been used as a musical instrument. It is possible that
the musical bow was adapted from it; if this process occurred, it
would explain the wide distribution of the musical instrument
without necessitating a historic relationship between it and other
stringed instruments.

Rattles and skin drums. The rattle, another instrument of almost universal distribution, was probably also invented independently in a great many cultures, since it could easily have
been patterned after nature. Dried gourds can be used as rattles,
with the seeds inside striking the shell, and primitive people may
have imitated them by devising other containers and replacing
the seeds with pebbles. On the other hand, it is probable that the
skin drum, which has a slightly less dense but nevertheless
world-wide distribution, was invented only once, because it is
relatively complex and is not related to other cultural or natural
phenomena.

DETERMINING THE AGE OF INSTRUMENTS

We have already seen that wide distribution of an instrumental
type may imply that it originated in remote times. The age of
instruments may also be partly determined by archeology. The
fact that archeologists have not uncovered any remains of a
certain instrument does not, of course, mean that the instrument
did not exist in antiquity, since not all materials of which instruments are constructed are capable of surviving very long. Those
made of wood, skin, and other organic substances have not ordinarily lasted. Instruments made of fired clay, which are usually
aerophones, have the best survival qualities. Panpipes and
whistles have been found in sites as old as two thousand years in
Peru and other parts of South America.[23]

The age of some folk and primitive instruments can be ascertained by examining similar forms in high cultures, where
written records of the instrument's history exist. It is evident that
cultivated instruments were often transmitted to the neighboring
less advanced cultures, where they were sometimes simplified,
and the reverse process occurred as ferquently. For example, the

aulos, a double-tubed reed instrument of the ancient Greeks, exists today in the high cultures of Arabia and Turkey and in the folk cultures of Greece and other Balkan countries, but it is not present any longer in Greek cultivated music. In this case the history of the instrument's migration can be clearly traced because the indigenous Balkan folk instrumental forms are ordinarily double-tubed recorders, not constructed of reeds. Ancient primitive instruments, like rattles, musical bows, and xylophones, have obviously been transmitted to the high cultures in which they are used today.

INSTRUMENT SYMBOLISM

The attempts of ethnomusicologists to discover the symbolism involved in primitive instruments have met with moderate success. The specialized roles of certain instruments in ritual and ceremony are widely recognized, although it is doubtful that the same instrument carries an identical symbolic meaning in different cultures. Genital symbolism is demonstrably present in some cultures, but it should not be assumed for all. The flute, drumstick, and single-slab xylophone are among the most common symbols for the male sex organ, while the drum symbolizes the female body. The sexual implications of these instruments are obvious in some cultures. In Polynesia, only women play single-slab xylophones;[24] whereas in most African cultures, only men are allowed to beat drums. Of course these examples are not typical of every situation; we have already described the African xylophones that are played by men. It is dangerous to assign universal symbolism to any instrument. Such a step is based on the erroneous notion that all primitive groups have similar attitudes, an unjustified assumption for any sort of cultural analysis. Even when instrumental symbolism is recognized by the primitive group itself, it is hardly ever verbalized — once in a while a culture possesses a formula that gives expression to the symbol, but such conscious manifestations are rare.

As we might have expected from the discussion of the functions of music in primitive cultures, musical instruments are very strongly associated with the supernatural. Sometimes certain instruments are considered sacred — in many parts of Africa, drums are regarded as deities. Primitive people often identify the sounds of instruments with the voices of supernatural beings. In some areas the noise of the bullroarer is thought to be the voices of ancestors; elsewhere (among the Plains Indians, for example) it symbolizes awesome natural phenomena like thunder. The use of instruments for signaling and other representations of language is sometimes connected with supernatural associations, as among the Ashanti of West Africa, who use drums to recite the history of their kingdom.[25]

The role of instruments in primitive cultures is thus not confined to musical performance per se. The instruments are ceremonial equipment, part of the group's religious paraphernalia. Some groups think of them as having distinct personalities; others consider them merely as material possessions. It is the symbolic aspect of instruments that gives them their status of importance, since the quantity of vocal music performed by primitive groups is far greater than the quantity of instrumental music.

American primitive music north of Mexico

Hitherto we have made comparisons of various stylistic traits in primitive music without any over-all systematic approach. They have been designed chiefly to show the kinds of contrasts and the great variety of material found in primitive cultures. It is impossible within the compass of this volume to give complete analyses of the music of all geographic areas, so one has been selected for detailed treatment: the music of the American aborigines north of Mexico.[1] North America has been chosen because for this continent there is available more musical material, in transcriptions and recordings, than for any other area of primitive culture comparable in size. The total population of the area in aboriginal times was relatively small, approximately one million. There were about one thousand tribes, which means that the average tribal population was one thousand; some tribes, indeed, consisted of only a few hundred people. The amount and variety of musical material at our disposal seems vast in view of the small number of participants. As we have pointed out before, an equally detailed survey of the music of Negro Africa would entail a much larger amount of information, since its population is around a hundred million.

In spite of this wealth of American material, comparative studies of tribes and areas on this continent are still infrequent. As we saw in Chapter 3, workers in the field have been largely absorbed in the necessary preliminary task of collecting the data. Comparative studies at an earlier date would have been premature; the one presented in this chapter, although it is based on a large number of songs from over eighty representative tribes, still rests on a mere sampling of material and will be subject to revision and enlargement for years to come.

We shall analyze the music of this region by dividing it into "music areas": geographic units whose inhabitants share a relatively homogeneous style that contrasts in important ways with the styles of surrounding areas. Music areas are patterned after the culture area concept. The first serious attempt to devise music areas for North America was a short paper published by Herzog in 1928,[2] in which he uses vocal technique and, to a lesser extent, melodic movement as the main criteria for area differentiation. Herzog does not give complete distributions of the traits he examines in this paper, but he does indicate a main line of demarcation between the northern and southern portions of the continent. In 1936, Helen Roberts published a more detailed study, *Musical Areas in Aboriginal North America.* Her monograph emphasizes the distribution of musical instruments rather than stylistic traits of vocal music, which after all comprises the bulk of primitive musical material. Much more information has been uncovered since her work was published. The conclusions drawn in this chapter agree in part with those of Roberts; but more material is included here, and the distribution of strictly musical phenomena is emphasized more than are culture areas as units of musical homogeneity.

In order to be designated a music area, a territory must include musical styles that hold in common one or more important traits, such as identical form types, scale types, or melodic ranges. As is true of division by culture areas, the marginal groups possess elements of both bordering regions. It is sometimes difficult to decide on the exact degree of homogeneity requisite to characterize a music area: areas of various sizes and levels may be designated — continents contrast with other continents, individual tribes with other individual tribes, etc. There are certain aspects of music common to the entire region north of Mexico that are not found on other continents, such as the virtual lack of polyphony (except for a few cases where it is incipient), the predominance of the pentatonic scale, and heterometric construction. But we shall present here six music areas within this continent, indicating how they differ from each other in significant ways. The areas are fairly large and agree approximately with the generally accepted culture areas of North America. The chief criterion used here in determining areas is the frequency of the various traits. Almost every trait occurs in every culture to some degree, because of the long-term intimate contact among the American primitive groups; therefore an area is defined by the traits prevalent in the majority of its songs, even though the same traits crop up sporadically and sparsely in other areas.

THE ESKIMO–NORTHWEST COAST MUSIC AREA

The first area to be discussed contains some of the simplest and some of the most complicated music in North America. It comprises three sub-areas that are distinguishable primarily because of their varying degrees of complexity. The music of the Eskimos is the simplest. The most complex sub-area is the Northwest Coast culture area, particularly the most culturally advanced tribes — the Kwakiutl, Nootka, Tsimshian, Makah, and Quileute. Occupying an intermediate position in regard to musical complexity are the Salish tribes directly east of the coast and extending to Oregon: the Thompson River Indians, the Bella Coola, the Sliamon, and others directly east of the Northwest Coast tribes.

The significant traits of Eskimo music are intensified in the music of the Salish tribes and even more so in the music of the Northwest Coast sub-area. Among these traits are recitative-like singing and the attendant complex rhythmic organization; relatively small melodic range, averaging about a sixth; and melodic prominence of major thirds and minor seconds, in contrast to the minor thirds and major seconds conspicuous in other areas. Among the Eskimos, melodic movement is undulating; among the Salish and Northwest Coast Indians it is pendulum-type, leaping in broad intervals from one limit of the range to the other. Example 50 illustrates Salish style.

The Northwest Coast music is among the most complicated on the continent, especially in regard to rhythmic structure. Percussive accompaniments to songs have rhythmic designs of their own, intricately related to the melody, and rigid percussion instruments are commonly used. In this sub-area, rudimentary polyphony has been discovered, although to my knowledge it has never been recorded. It consists either of a drone or of parallelism at various intervals.[3] Antiphonal and responsorial forms are also used. Pulsation and vocal tension characterize the style of singing, although these are typical of several other music areas too. The extreme tension in the vocal chords produces dynamic contrast, ornamentation, and rhythmic pulsation: sudden accents without special articulation may occur several times during one sustained note. This may be responsible for the sharp contrasts between very long and very short tones.

THE GREAT BASIN MUSIC AREA

Most of the desert tribes of Utah and Nevada are part of the Great Basin music area, as are some tribes in southern Oregon. The most familiar tribal names here are the Paiute, Ute, and Shoshoni of the Basin, and the Modoc and Klamath of Oregon. This area is sparsely settled, with a population slightly over 10 per cent of that of the Eskimo-Northwest Coast music area. Its music is not nearly so well known. The style is extremely simple; it has small melodic ranges averaging barely over a perfect fifth, many tetronic scales, and very short forms. Most songs are iterative, with each phrase repeated once, although songs with multiple repetitions are found occasionally. The Modoc and Klamath Indians have many songs that consist of only one repeated phrase, and many of their scales are ditonic and tritonic. Example 51 typifies the Great Basin style.

In the late nineteenth century, the Great Basin style was carried to many tribes of the Great Plains and surrounding areas by the Ghost Dance religion.[4] This cult, which originated among the Paiute, arose in reaction against the white supremacy that was forcing the aboriginal cultures to dwindle. It taught that if a particular dance were performed, all whites would die and all dead Indians return to life. The ceremony spread from the Great Basin and with it went the style of the songs, which is characterized by paired-phrase patterns very strongly and by a relaxed, nonpulsating vocal technique. Thus the Plains Ghost Dance songs were originally part of the tradition of the Great Basin music area.

Herzog describes another group of songs that are related to the Great Basin area, albeit somewhat less closely.[5] The group consists of many of the lullabies, songs from tales, and gambling songs that are sung all over the continent, and is characterized by its great simplicity. It is this quality that relates it to the Great Basin, together with other more concrete features. Some scholars believe that these songs are survivals from a really archaic layer of music; and it may well be that the entire Great Basin style is also a remnant of ancient days, protected from acculturation by its relatively isolated cultural position.

THE CALIFORNIA-YUMAN MUSIC AREA

The California-Yuman music area consists of most of California and part of Arizona, and includes such tribes as the Pomo and Miwok of central California,[6] the Luiseno, Catalineno, and Gabrielino of southern California, and the Yuman tribes — the Mohave, Yuman, Havasupai, Maricopa, and others. This area is characterized chiefly by one striking trait: the presence of the rise (see page 73) in almost all of its songs. The vocal technique of the area is relaxed and nonpulsating, resembling some of the techniques of Western cultivated music. Other significant traits are the use of a fairly large amount of isometric material, some isorhythmic tendencies, simple rhythmic organization, pentatonic scales without half tones and with an average range of an octave, sequences, and syncopated figures like the following.

The use of the rise by these tribes exemplifies particularly well how the frequent occurrence of one trait can determine the boundaries of a music area. The forms of the rise are not necessarily identical throughout the area. Usually the rise contains new melodic material and is related to the non-rise parts of the song by virtue of the rhythmic structure. In some instances, the tones used in the rise are no higher in pitch than the highest tones of the non-rise portion; but the rise is nonetheless distinct because it includes a much greater number of the high-pitched tones. The relationship between the rise and the non-rise portions of a song form varies considerably from tribe to tribe. In central California the non-rise portion is usually a single reiterated phrase, a litany-type form, with the rise consisting of the same melodic material transposed up an octave. Among the Yuman tribes, the non-rise portion consists of longer repeated units, each comprising several phrases, while the rise usually consists of a single unit of three to five phrases that is rendered only once. In southern California the forms tend to be progressive, although the two just described are also found. Example 52 illustrates a complex form of the rise used by the Arizona Yuman Indians.

THE PLAINS-PUEBLO MUSIC AREA

The Plains-Pueblo area is the largest geographically and the third largest in population. It occupies the central portion of the United States, roughly coinciding with the Louisiana Purchase but extending farther to the southwest. At one time its musical style was supposed to be racially inherent in the Indians and shared by all of them.[7] This premise was assumed because most of the Indian material available early in the twentieth century came from the Plains-Pueblo area. Even today this area is by far the best documented, and the sampling of tribes presented here is more extensive than for the other areas.

The chief musical traits of the entire area are extreme vocal tension and pulsation, with resulting ornamentation; tile-type melodic contour; relatively complex rhythm, including the use of several durational values per song; and a type of form that we call the "incomplete repetition type." This form consists of two large sections, the second being an incomplete rendition of the first; the first phrase of the first section is also frequently repeated. Typical schemes are ABC, BC and AABC, ABC. Each large section has tile-type contour. The form is governed by the textual structure; the first half of the text is composed of meaningless syllables, and the second half, sung with the incomplete musical repetition, is meaningful. Example 29 is a typical song of the Plains-Pueblo music area.

A number of songs from other music areas are found in the Plains-Pueblo repertories. This is true of all music areas but especially noticeable here because of the central location of the Plains-Pueblo area, which is contiguous to all the others. We find, for example, Great Basin songs — lullabies, songs from tales, gambling and Ghost Dance songs — and Peyote songs that originated among the southern Athabascans.

This area is so large and well documented that it is possible to identify five sub-areas, units with relatively homogeneous styles that contrast with each other but have in common the characteristics mentioned above. The easternmost sub-area is around Lake Superior and Lake Michigan, and includes the Ojibwa, Menomini, and Winnebago Indians. The musical style is differentiated from the others by particularly large melodic ranges (averaging over a twelfth) and by the use of isorhythmic material in at least one-third of all songs, a larger proportion than elsewhere. Some songs are entirely isorhythmic, others have isorhythmic segments or slightly modified isorhythmic patterns.

Directly south of these tribes, in Missouri, Kansas, and Nebraska, the tribes of the Southern Prairies culture area constitute another sub-area. These tribes, primarily the Pawnee, Osage, and Omaha, are related somewhat more closely to the tribes of the southeastern United States in musical style than are the other Plains-Pueblo tribes. Their forms are more complex, often consisting of several short sections interwoven in iterative and reverting relationships. The average range is smaller than in the music area as a whole, and the scales are likely to have more tones — tetratonic scales are rare, hexatonic relatively common.

The most typical sub-area, and in some ways the simplest in style, comprises the central Plains tribes. It is evidently under less influence from other music areas than are the other sub-areas. The main tribes are the Blackfoot, Crow, Dakota, Cheyenne, Arapaho, Kiowa, and Comanche, stretching in one line just east of the Rocky Mountains from Canada into Texas. The material here is characterized by extreme pulsation and vocal tension, a preference for perfect fourths in the melody, rhythmic complexity, and a relative proponderance of tetratonic scales. These traits are intensified in the center of the area, among the Arapaho and Cheyenne. The range of the songs averages about a tenth. In the northern part, particularly among the Blackfoot, the material is simpler, the ranges smaller, and the scales have fewer tones, while in the southern part the influence of tribes in the southeastern and southwestern United States is evident, causing greater complexity and variety. In the Plains, too, the relationship between percussive accompaniment and the melody is not constant; drum beats coincide only approximately with the important durational values of the melody, resulting in an apparently discordant relationship.

The sub-area most complex in musical style is that of the Pueblo of New Mexico and Arizona, including the Hopi, Zuñi, Taos, San Ildefonso, Santo Domingo, and many others. The style here is one of the most complex on the continent and differs most markedly from the rest of the Plains-Pueblo styles. The songs tend to be much longer and to have more variety in form and melodic contour. The types of percussive accompaniment are more varied and they occasionally have rhythmic designs related to those of the melody. The ranges are between an octave and a twelfth, and the rhythmic complexity is about equal to that of the Plains sub-area. The scales tend to have more tones than they do elsewhere on the continent — hexatonic and heptatonic scales are common. The most complex songs are the Katchina dance songs, sung by masked dancers impersonating clan ancestors. The most complex varieties of the Pueblo style are found in the western part of the sub-area, in Hopi and Zuñi material, while the eastern Pueblos, including the Tanoans and Keresans, partake of a simpler style intermediate in complexity between those of the Plains and the western Pueblos.

The Pima and Papago tribes, located in southern Arizona, are marginal in style, having traits of both the Plains-Pueblo and the California-Yuman music areas. Their melodic movement and vocal technique are similar to that of the Yumans, although they do not have the rise, while their forms and rhythmic materials are related to those of the Pueblos. A detailed comparison of Pima and Pueblo styles has been made by Herzog.[8]

THE ATHABASCAN MUSIC AREA

The Athabascan area is unusual in several ways: it is the least known and least documented, and it is composed of two separated segments, a northern and a southern one, thus making it the sole broken-up music area on the continent. It takes its name from the Athabascan language family, with which it coincides almost exactly. The northern Athabascans occupy the inland of western Canada and Alaska; the southern Athabascans are the Apache and Navaho of the southwestern United States.[9] The music of the Navaho is the best known in the area, while the Apache music has been documented sketchily and the music of the northern Athabascans is hardly known at all. In fact, the inclusion of the northern Athabascans in the area should be considered highly tentative, for it is based on very scanty material. The Athabascan style in general is one of the simplest on the continent, perhaps the simplest next to the Great Basin style.

The southern Athabascan style is characterized chiefly by the limited number of durational values, usually no more than two to a song. The rhythmic organization is also simple in other respects. The typical melodic contour is arc-type. The melodic range is wide, especially among the Navaho, and the melodic intervals tend to be large: major and minor thirds and perfect fourths and fifths predominate, while leaps of an octave are not rare. Broad acrobatic maneuvers in the melody are characteristic. As a result, the scales usually have few tones; tritonic and tetratonic scales are very common, usually occurring in triad-like formation. The typical southern Athabascan song form is strophic. The vocal technique is characterized by pulsation, vocal tension, and falsetto — these occur here more than in the areas discussed thus far; excepting the Plains-Pueblo area. Example 53 is a typical Navaho song.

The northern Athabascan style, to judge from the few available samples, seems to be similar, but it has apparently been considerably influenced by the styles of the Eskimo–Northwest Coast and the Plains-Pueblo music areas.

The Peyote songs found primarily in the Plains-Pueblo area are evidently related to the Athabascan area also, both stylistically and historically. The Peyote religion was spread among the Plains-Pueblo tribes by the Apaches, either directly or deviously. Some Apache musical traits carried over into the Plains-Pueblo adaptations of the Peyote songs. The songs are now composites of both styles: they have the two durational values and the predominant thirds and fifths of the Apaches, plus the tile-type melodic contour, incomplete repetitions, and isorhythmic tendencies characteristic of Plains-Pueblo music. The Peyote vocal technique is closer to the Athabascan than to the Plains-Pueblo one, and the Peyote cadential formula may be another Athabascan feature.

THE EASTERN MUSIC AREA

The section of the continent between the Mississippi River and the Atlantic makes up the Eastern music area. The music of the entire area is not well known; only the southeastern part and the Atlantic Coast are musically well documented. The tribes of the Southeast, and the Iroquois, who are related linguistically to some of them, have the most complex style; they include the Creek, Yuchi, Cherokee, and Choctaw. The Algonquian-speaking tribes, such as the Delaware and Penobscot, have simpler music. The Shawnee, although Algonquian, have lived so close to the southeastern tribes that their style is relatively complex. Their position and its historical implications are discussed in detail in Chapter 10.

The main musical characteristics of the Eastern area are short phrases in iterative and reverting relationships; the use of shouts before, during, and after songs; pentatonic scales without half tones; simple rhythmic and metric organization; and, probably most important, a great deal of antiphonal and responsorial technique with the accompanying rudimentary imitative polyphony. The melodic movement is usually unspecialized and tends to be gradually descending. A moderate amount of pulsation and vocal tension is present. Example 54 illustrates the music of the Eastern area.

A knowledge of the aboriginal populations of these music areas is useful in correlating population with complexity of style. The following list was compiled from estimates given by Kroeber,[10] which are, in turn, based on those of Mooney.

Eastern	275,000
Eskimo – Northwest Coast	267,000
Plains-Pueblo	250,000
California-Yuman	125,000
Athabascan	90,000
Great Basin	30,000

The three areas largest both in size and population contain the three centers of greatest musical complexity: the Gulf of Mexico in the Eastern area, the Northwest Coast, and the Pueblos. The smaller areas contain the simpler styles, whose simplicity correlates almost exactly with the size of the population.

The music areas of North America partially coincide with the culture areas of the continent.[11] The Eskimo–Northwest Coast music area contains the two culture areas from which it takes its name, and the Great Basin music area covers the same territory as the Great Basin culture area (or sub-area, according to Kroeber's scheme). The boundaries do not usually match so closely; some music areas contain parts of several culture areas. The California-Yuman music area, although compact in itself, contains parts of the Southwest culture area as well as California. Conversely, the Southwest culture area contains parts of the

California-Yuman, the Athabascan, and the Plains-Pueblo music areas. This type of arrangement is the rule throughout the continent. In both music and culture areas, the diversity of traits is greater in the western part of the continent than in the eastern. The western half is also divided into more areas than the eastern.

The correlation of music areas with linguistic families or linguistic structural types is less pronounced than with cultural units. The only close correlation is found in the Athabascan music area, where almost all tribes speak only the Athabascan languages. An area as homogeneous in musical style as the Plains-Pueblo includes tribes speaking the Athabascan, Algonquian, Siouan, Uto-Aztecan, and Kiowa languages.

Certain traits of Indian music, especially some rather specialized ones, have a distribution that is interesting. These traits are also relevant to the reconstruction of the history of Indian music. Among them are incomplete-repetition form, polyphony, tense vocal technique, and the rise, which we shall use as an example here. The rise is characteristic of the California-Yuman area, where it occurs in the majority of the songs, but it is also found elsewhere in other varieties and with less frequency. The specific form of the rise tends to agree with the fundamental principles of each area where it occurs; for example, on the Northwest Coast the rise is used with variation and iteration, which are characteristic of the area as a whole. In the southeastern United States, forms using the rise tend to include the reverting relationships that are common there. The rise is found in about 20 per cent of the music of the Northwest Coast sub-area of the Eskimo –Northwest Coast music area. It is present in about 15 per cent of the songs in the southeastern United States and in a few songs farther north in the Eastern area. The proportion differs in every tribe, and the sampling on which these estimates are based may not be accurate, but it is probable that these percentages indicate at least the relative ferquencies within the tribes.

CHRONOLOGICAL DEVELOPMENT OF AMERICAN INDIAN MUSIC

Thus far our discussion of North American primitive music has been on a purely descriptive and comparative level, with no attempt at historical explanation. Reconstructing the history of this music by examining musical traits primarily, without much consideration of the history of the cultures and the migrations of the tribes, would seem rather bold. Nevertheless, we shall undertake this reconstruction. Needless to say, it must be highly tentative, for there is very little besides logic to validate the results from the standpoint of music history, and there is only a small amount of ethno-historical evidence available with which to test them. However, it is probable that music areas are historical units in some sense, and that they represent relatively separate movements and perhaps historical periods. Exact dates or even approximate periods in terms of years cannot, of course, be given. Any kind of chronology can be presented only in terms of the relative development of the music areas. We can attempt to put the events of music history in chronological order, but we can do nothing whatever about dating them unless they took place in the last few centuries.

Of the North American styles known at the present time, the oldest is probably that of the Great Basin area. Its age is attested to by its relative simplicity and by the fact that its style is represented throughout the continent in lullabies, gambling songs, and songs from tales. Similar styles are found throughout the Old World in widely scattered musical cultures of great simplicity. The period during which this style was common to all of North America antedates the development of advanced cultures in Mexico, Middle America, and Peru. On this style were superimposed others, and it has remained dominant only in the isolated and culturally simple Great Basin.

With the development of the advanced cultures in Mexico came a style characterized by relaxed vocal technique and probably by the rise. Whether this style still exists in Mexico or whether it was replaced there before the advent of the white man cannot be ascertained now, because we know so little of Mexico Indian music, especially that of the advanced cultures. At any rate, this style spread northward, particularly along the coasts. It is the basis for the styles of the California-Yuman and the Eastern areas. Besides the rise, these areas have in common relative rhythmic simplicity, isometric material, pentatonic scales without half tones (to a greater extent than elsewhere), and forms consisting of short sections. The differences between their styles are probably due to later contacts with other music areas. Whether the Mexican style spread into the central part of the continent, including Texas and environs, we cannot conjecture. If it did, it was later replaced by the Plains-Pueblo style.

At about the same time, three separate waves of musical style reached North America from Asia. They had a number of traits in common, notably tense and pulsating vocal technique. All three came across the Bering Strait, and their influence is evident today in the styles of some of the Paleo-Siberian tribes, like the Chuckchee, Yukaghir, Koryak, and others in the extreme east of Siberia.[12] The three styles are represented in the Plains-Pueblo, Athabascan, and Eskimo – Northwest Coast areas, and may have come to America in that order. They spread south on the continent and eventually came in contact with the movements initiated in Mexico. It is at the southernmost points of all three areas that the most complex material is found: on the Northwest Coast, in the Pueblos, and among the Navaho. Contact between the Northwest Coast and Mexico seems implausible because of the great geographic distance and the intervening Great Basin style, yet the presence of concrete musical phenomena like bird-shaped whistles in both areas is evidence that it did take place. Since the Navaho were undoubtedly the last of these peoples to reach the South (they did so probably no more than eight hundred years ago), they probably had no direct contact with the Mexican movements but were influenced indirectly by way of the Pueblos.

The Plains-Pueblo area extended throughout the central part of the continent, influencing the surrounding areas and imparting much of its tense vocal technique to the Eastern area. This process continues today: tribes of all areas are learning Plains songs whenever contact exists, but the Plains Indians rarely learn songs from tribes whose musical styles are unrelated to theirs.

Thus, the three centers of musical complexity — the Pueblos, the Northwest Coast, and the southeastern United States — although they all represent mixtures of northern and Mexican elements, consist of different combinations. The Pueblos have the culmination of the northern elements; the Gulf of Mexico, with its cultural similarity to ancient Mexico and its use of polyphony, shows the Mexican influence predominantly. The Northwest Coast probably represents a mixture of Mexican and northern elements, with polyphony being the chief Mexican contribution.

We infer that these centers of complexity are points of contact rather than centers of diffusion, because of their geographic position within their music areas. They are more likely to be at the geographic extremes, especially the southern extremes, than in the center. This is true, of course, of the Pueblos, the tribes in the Gulf of Mexico (within the Eastern area), the Navaho (within the Athabascan area), and the Northwest Coast tribes (who are at the southwestern limit of their area). In culture areas, centers of complexity have usually been interpreted differently, since they tend to be at the geographic centers of the areas.

Finally, it should be emphasized again that not only the historical recapitulation presented above but also the classifications of the tribes in music areas are highly tentative and subject to revision. Very little is yet known about North American Indian music, although relatively more than is know about primitive music on other continents, and very few tribes are known intimately. Many of the tribes have disintegrated, and there is no hope now of ever discovering their musical traits.

9

African and new world Negro music

Up to this point, we have treated primitive music as an isolated phenomenon. Its connections, both remote and immediate, with other realms of music have been mentioned but not described in any detail. This chapter will be devoted to the study of a group of primitive styles that have invaded both folk and sophisticated cultures of a foreign area in relatively recent times — Negro music in the New World.

There are several ways in which musical styles migrate. In anthropological theory, all of them fall into the category of acculturation, that is, the culture of one society being superimposed on the individuals of another one that is geographically close. Acculturation has taken place in practically all areas of primitive culture. Wherever the white man has colonized it has occurred, with great intensity in some places and with but little impact in others. The currents nearly always move from the advanced to the primitive group; primitive peoples have taken on the ways of Western civilization, while only a few customs of primitive peoples have found their way into modern Europe and America. Musical acculturation occurs in various ways. Sometimes two musical styles become intertwined, so that a single song contains characteristics of both of them; sometimes new material is added to a repertory. The latter is the case among most North American Indian tribes: although many Indians have learned the songs of the whites and know them along with their older songs, one rarely encounters musical material among them that cannot be definitely labeled as originally either white or Indian. The other type of musical acculturation, a mixture of styles in the repertory, is found in American Negro music and in Spain, where folk music was somewhat influenced by the Arabic invasions in the Middle Ages. There is a definite difference between the methods of transfer of the Spanish and the Afro-American musical material, however. Whereas the indigenous Spanish folk music was influenced by an invading culture, the Afro-American material represents the acculturation of a technically "invading" group, the American Negroes, by Occidental influence. In other words, after their transfer to North and Middle America, the Negroes largely took on the musical styles of the white men and mixed them with elements of their own.

The American Negro material — including South and Middle American music as well as West Indian — is probably the largest body of music to come under Occidental influence, and has doubtless also transformed Western styles more greatly than has any other primitive musical corpus. Wherever it has gone, it has had its effect on folk music, on popular music in the form of jazz, and on a good deal of cultivated music (often indirectly through folk material). The influence of both folk and cultivated Western music on Negro music has also been great. Thus we find in the Americas a group of Negro styles composed of African and European elements that have evidently been compatible, a group that is a unique combination of traits and whose impact on the musical world of the last several decades has been tremendous.

THE BACKGROUND OF AFRICAN MUSIC

In order to indicate at least tentatively which elements in Afro-American music are African and which European, we must give a brief outline of the background of African Negro music. Contrary to the contention of some scholars, Africa has not been musically isolated; it has undergone importations of musical material from several known sources, in both remote and recent times. We have already discussed the importation of the xylophone from Indonesia around 500 A.D. This evidently revolutionized African music at the time, if we judge from the important place of the xylophone in Africa today. Other practices, such as the use of xylophones in orchestras, may have been imported from the advanced Javanese and Balinese cultures. The effects of the Mohammedan invasion of North Africa in the seventh century were evidently felt along the East Coast and in West Africa, for today we find Arabic elements in Negro material that is otherwise completely different. They consist of monophonic, chant-like singing, with ornamenation, unclear rhythm, small intervals, and occasionally harp accompaniment. These Arabic elements are found today in some tribes south of the East Horn, like the Watusi.

European influence has been most recent, but there was probably early contact also. The similarity of the African material to European folk music has been mentioned before. Both styles have in common diatonic and pentatonic scales, certain types of polyphony (found less frequently in Europe), and a tendency towards isometric organization (found in some African areas). The similarities are often rather vague, but African primitive and European folk music does represent a relatively homogeneous block that contrasts with the primitive music in some other areas, like that of the American Indians. The similar types of polyphony are based on parallel fourths and fifths and are found in Central Asia and East Africa. The connection between these two large areas is probably prehistoric and is certainly pre-Islamic, since they are separated by the broad belt of Arabic music that runs across North Africa and the Near East. Since a great deal of African Negro culture evidently was originally diffused from Egypt and the Near East,[1] and since much of Western culture also originated there, this area may be the original home of those stylistic features that African and European folk music have in common. Another suggestion has been offered by Leo Frobenius,[2] who postulates a prehistoric connection between southern Europe and Africa. His theory is largely based on the prehistoric European and more recent Bushman styles of rock painting. At any rate, the similarity of African and European traditional styles may have assisted their assimilation in the New World.

More recently, the influence of European musical styles on African music has been caused by European colonization. The combination of European folk and popular tunes with African techniques of drumming and performance is demonstrated by Example 55, the song "Frère Jacques," which was recorded among the Ibo of Nigeria.

Although music areas have not yet been devised for Africa, it is possible to correlate some styles with large geographic areas. Generally speaking, West African rhythmic material is differentiated from East African by greater rhythmic complexity and more heterometric tendencies. In East and South Africa, although the rhythm remains relatively complex, it tends to be organized isometrically. Polyphony is present throughout Negro Africa, with similar forms in both East and West. The intervals used in the East, however, tend to be fourths and fifths, while the West prefers thirds. The tendency towards these intervals is present not only in the harmonic structure but also in the melodic line. Melodic movement is usually undulating or gradually descending, occasionally arc-shaped. According to Kolinski, a preference for series of thirds in the melody and an absence of minor seconds mark West African music.[3] Thus we find that heterometric rhythm, rhythmic polyphony, thirds both melodic and harmonic, and lack of minor seconds are typical of West Africa, in contrast to the fifths, the use of seconds in the melody, and the isometric and somewhat simpler rhythmic structure that are common in the East. We may conclude from this that East African music is somewhat closer than West African to European folk material, an interesting deduction in view of the possible accumulation of Egyptian and North African culture by the East Africans in prehistoric times.

The influence of African music on Western has been largely due to the enslavement of Negroes and their transportation to Europe and the New World. In Europe throughout the Middle Ages there were few Negroes, but as early as the sixteenth century a Negro settlement in Naples may have had an effect on Orlando di Lasso, some of whose "Moresche" were evidently influenced by Negroes.[4] The bulk of the slaves went, of course, to America, where they were widely scattered and exist today in a number of groups whose cultures differ significantly. There are many Negroes in Brazil, in French, British, and Dutch (Surinam) Guiana, and throughout the West Indies, with the largest numbers in Haiti (whose population is almost entirely Negro), Cuba, Jamaica, Trinidad, the Virgin Islands, and the Gulla Islands off the coast of Georgia. In North America the Negro is found largely in the southeastern United States and in the urban areas of the East and Midwest. Most New World Negroes came from West Africa, primarily from the smaller tribes whose members were captured by armies of the large kingdoms, such as Ashanti and Dahomey, and were sold to the European slave traders. Consequently the study of African influences in New World Negro music, and comparisons of New World with African material, hinge primarily on our knowledge of West African music.

THE ORIGINS OF NEW WORLD NEGRO MUSIC

In the following paragraphs various theories concerning the origin of New World Negro styles will be discussed and criticized, some musical material will be examined, and conclusions drawn. Debates among the representatives of differing points of view have been bitter, although we hope to reconcile them and to take the useful facets from all. The controversies have frequently been characterized by unwillingness to compromise and by a certain negligence in defining terms and problems. They have centered primarily on Negro music in the United States, where the most acculturation took place; West Indian and South American material present no great difficulty, since practically all scholars agree that it retains very largely its original African traits.

South American Negro music. Students of South American Negro materials have usually been content to point out African survivals. The most solid study in this area is Kolinski's on Surinam music.[5] Kolinski, whose knowledge of West African music is probably superior to anyone else's, gives three traits as most typical of that area: heterometric construction, the use of melodic thirds, particularly in chains, and the lack of half steps (semitones). He divides the Surinam material into two sections. The first is found among the so-called Bush Negroes, a group of slaves who escaped early to the inland jungle and lived a primitive existence there, very similar to their life in Africa; almost all of their songs have the three typical West African traits. The second section is the music of the urban Negroes who inhabit the coast. Only about one fourth of all their songs include the three traits: 31 per cent of the religious, 10 per cent of the secular, and 13 per cent of the songs in tales have them. The magnitude of the survivals in the religious material is interesting. It is born out in other New World areas also; it accords with the association of music with religion that is prevalent among primitive peoples; and it illustrates the widespread conservatism of religious music, which is demonstrable in many cultures, including that of Western Europe.

Further study of West Indian and South American Negro music has not been of great theoretical value, since the question of the extent of African survivals has been more or less settled. In general, the West Indian and Brazilian musical material is considered to be more African than that of the United States.

Survivalism. Theoretical discussions about African influences in Negro music in the United States have abounded, despite the sparsity of accurate transcriptions to substantiate the theories. We shall take up here four general theories about the origin of this music: survivalism, syncretism, nonsurvivalism, and the compromise theory.

The survival of African cultural traits in the New World has been of great interest to anthropologists. Melville J. Herskovits has been one of the leading scholars in this field; his interests range from physical anthropology and general culture to language and folklore, encompassing music. His student, Richard Waterman, has applied Herskovits' methods to the study of New World Negro music. These scholars have aimed primarily at identifying so-called "Africanisms" — remnants of African culture in the New World. Comparison of the intensity of Africanisms in various locations, and of the areas of living in which

Africanisms are present, forms the basis for the theories of diffusion and acculturation that the survivalist school has constructed. Music has played an important part in their investigations because of its wide appeal. Herskovits has constructed a scale of the intensity of New World Africanisms,[6] which indicates the greatest amount of African survival in several aspects of culture. His scale includes every area of Negro population in the New World. It shows that music may be the most African aspect of New World Negro culture; it is marked "very" or "quite" African in all cases, whereas for other aspects of culture, African traits have survived with less intensity. It is also interesting to note that Africanisms are stronger by far in those aspects that are related to music, like art, folklore, and language, or in which music plays a role, like religion, than they are in those aspects that are related more closely to economic structure and social organization. These last aspects require more acculturation if a group is to exist comfortably in a foreign culture.

Apparent survivals of African cultural traits are not always interpreted by critics of the Herskovits group as being African in origin. Other schools of thought explain these survivals in terms of the new social and economic position of the Negro in his New World environment. For example, the mother is an important and superior figure in Southern Negro families. Survivalists explain her status by relating it to the matrilineal descent of some West African tribes; other scholars trace it to the frequent absence from home of the father because of working conditions, or to promiscuity and the resulting fatherless home. The view that apparent Africanisms are due to new social and economic factors has important connotations for some of the theories about American Negro folk music.

The survivalists believe that most of the New World Negro musical material available is originally African. Some adherents of the school go so far as to point out actual tunes that they believe were transplanted from Africa. Although no actual proof has been given, there is a remote possibility that they are right. Most of the survivalists try to indicate the presence of basic African characteristics in the music of the New World, from which they conclude that some traits of this music are completely African. Waterman, for example, believes that the chief African trait of American Negro music is the rhythmic structure. He thinks that "hot" rhythm was carried from African music into American folk music and jazz.[7] He defines hot rhythm mainly by intuitive and subjective identifications, such as describing the rhythm as "compelling"; translated into technical terms, it means primarily syncopation and anticipation of the beat over a steady pulse, usually provided by drums. He believes that the importance of rhythmic instruments in African culture, plus the essentially rhythmic quality of melodic instruments like the xylophone, helped carry into New World Negro music a preoccupation with rhythmic phenomena.

Besides Herskovits and Waterman, the survivalist school includes scholars who have been interested primarily in popular music. Especially notable is Rudi Blesh, whose book on the history of jazz is probably the best and most exhaustive to date.[8]

Syncretism. Waterman has also applied the theory of syncretism to New World Negro music.[9] Syncretism is the presence of similar or analogous traits in two cultures that are becoming acculturated; the similarity of the indigenous traits in each original group assures the survival, to some extent, of the trait in the acculturated group. For example, we find West African religious concepts better preserved in Roman Catholic areas than in Protestant. The reason for this is the similarity between the West African religions, with their many deities at various levels of importance, and Roman Catholicism, with its many saints. In Haiti, for example, the African *loa* (deities) live on identified as Catholic saints after acculturation; some saints retain the characteristics of the *loa*, and where the *loa* remain separate entities in the African cults, they often acquire a likeness to the saints. In Protestant countries, where saints are not important, the African religious concepts have usually not survived.[10] There also seems to be in general a higher intensity of African survivals in the music of Negro groups who have settled in Roman Catholic cultures where Romance languages are spoken than in the music of the Negroes who have settled in Protestant, English-speaking cultures.

Applying the theory of syncretism to New World Negro music, Waterman tries to explain why Africanisms have survived whereas other primitive cultures that have come in contact with the West have not had similar carry-overs. His explanation is the existence of two basic and similar traits in both European and African styles: polyphony and the diatonic scale. Because of these strong resemblances, the African versions of these traits should presumably survive after acculturation has taken place.

Nonsurvivalism. The outstanding figure among the nonsurvivalists is George Pullen Jackson, whose main interest is not African material but the folk music, especially the religious folk music, of the American whites. Jackson has traced the history of the spiritual and has concluded that it originated in the Scotch-Irish and English folk hymnody of the South.[11] He is not interested in the detailed transcription of traditional material or in the study of performance and stylistic technique. He is most concerned with the identification of specific tunes, occasionally of melodic skeletons, which he accomplishes mainly by using historical sources, ignoring the methods of ethnomusicology. He traces Negro spirituals to white hymnbooks of the nineteenth century and concludes that the Negroes learned the hymns from the whites mainly between 1820 and 1860, the time of the greatest flourishing of slavery in the South. He believes therefore that all the religious Negro music in the United States is borrowed white material.

Jackson does not take into account such recognizably African traits as antiphonal technique, special kinds of sound production, and percussive accompaniment. He is limited by his method, for these traits are not of course mentioned in most historical sources, but within this limitation, his conclusions stand to reason. Less conscientious nonsurvivalists have used the relatively simple culture of the Negroes and their inferior status in America as the basis for prejudice against Negro music. Such an approach must obviously be condemned as nonobjective, since racial and economic background can be demonstrated to have no correlation with musical aptitude, quality, and complexity. While Jackson's findings are accepted by all serious scholars, those conclusions that resemble his but based on racial and cultural prejudice must be rejected.

A compromise theory. The main tenet of the middle-of-the-road school of thought on Afro-American music is that the difference between the survivalists and the nonsurvivalists is not one of fundamental assumptions or interpretations but one of emphasis. The survivalists, according to this school, are mainly concerned with tracing stylistic elements, ordinarily not transmitted in the notations of historical sources; the nonsurvivalists are concerned with tracing the origins of individual melodies and melody-types, regardless of the manner of their performance. Among the first ethnomusicologists to utilize both approaches was Hornbostel. He tried to determine whether the songs, especially the spirituals, of the Negroes were essentially "African" or "European." [12] When he found that they could not be definitely categorized as either, he decided that the style originated with the Negroes after they came to America. While this forthright statement may be considered somewhat naïve in terms of modern anthropological theory, he was certainly justified in stressing the originality of the combination that the American Negroes had built from both elements. The main point of view of the compromise theorists today is similar to Hornbostel's; they do not hold that the melodies of the American Negroes originated in Africa, but assume that the Negroes have taken over tunes of the whites and combined with them African stylistic traits — hot rhythm, much variation, preference for part-singing, antiphony and response. Whether the Negroes have selected European material that would fit naturally with these traits is not known — such choices would not be very difficult to make, considering the wealth of appropriate tunes.

NEW WORLD NEGRO MUSIC TODAY

All of these schools of thought have contributed positively to reconstructing the history of Afro-American music, and all are scholastically sound, although the compromise solution is probably closest to the truth. In the following paragraphs we will examine a few cases of Negro music in various parts of the New

World and illustrate the gradual transition from predominantly African materials in the West Indies to slightly Africanized Western songs in the United States.

The largest body of African survivals probably exists today in Haiti. An entire complex of West African religions has been fused into a group of cults called the Vodun, in which each cult — Ibo, Nago, Quitta Mouille, etc. — is named after a West African tribe and has its own music.[13] The songs are characterized by pentatonic scales without half tones, extensive use of thirds, often in triadic form, and a harsh, tense vocal technique that differs from that used by most American Indians but is found in Africa. As in Africa, antiphonal and responsorial techniques are ever present, and women frequently lead in singing. In fact, except for the virtual absence of polyphony, the Vodun material closely resembles African styles — even some of the melodies may have originated in Africa. Example 56 gives a typical Haitian melody without a drum accompaniment.

Drumming is a vital part of many Vodun songs. There are always three male drummers,[14] who perform with instruments of different size and pitch. Each cult has a characteristic drum rhythmic pattern, so that the cult to which a song belongs can be determined by its percussive accompaniment. Example 57 gives fragments from two songs of different Vodun cults. Most of the songs are used to accompany dancing. According to Harold Courlander, "the singing leader begins a song by beating time with a rattle, and sings a song once or twice before the dancers take up the melody. When the rhythm is clearly indicated in the song, the player of the small drum begins; he is followed after a moment by the middle drummer, and last of all by the player of the large drum. Then the dancing begins." [15]

The music of the Bahamas has become more acculturated. Hot rhythm is absent. Bahaman polyphony exists largely in the African form of individual deviations by singers within a chorus, but it utilizes progressions from European harmony. The spiritual "Hallie Rock" (Example 58) is typical: one chorus moves in melodic seconds, one in thirds, another in perfect fifths — the essentials of the Western tonic-dominant progression. The practice of allowing one voice to rest on a long note while the others are active is a remnant of its original antiphonal form. "Hallie Rock" is litany-type in structure, with a single short section repeated many times; the vocal quality evident on the recording from which the transcription was made is singularly harsh. Example 59 is an antiphonal song from the Bahamas, with rudimentary polyphony shown in the places where the two vocal parts briefly overlap.

In the United States we find two separate types of Negro music: folk songs and jazz. The folk songs belong primarily to the Negroes of the rural South. Their form, which includes both Africanisms and traits strictly European in origin, is usually simple, although this prevalent clarity has been somewhat obscured in the popular mind by the individual, deviant styles of such well-known singers as Huddy Ledbetter and Josh White. Example 60 is a fragment from a "blues" song — a type noted for lyrical quality and tragic text. Its scale is pentatonic without half tones, and the melodic line is strikingly non-Western in its direct descent. In its tone system and ornamentation, the song closely resembles the Anglo-American folk style, but the melodic lines of the latter are more frequently arc-shaped and its rhythms do not include anticipation of the beat. The African elements of Example 60, then, consist of hot rhythm and descending contour. Aside from the slow, lyrical spirituals, which have been popularized, there are other Negro religious songs that exhibit unmistakably African traits. A type known as the ring shout, often sung during dancing, uses polyphony, responsorial technique with individual variation, and percussive accompaniment. Many rhymes used by children at play are sung or chanted in African-like rhythms.

Jazz and its various offspring — swing, bebop, etc. — have been adopted to a great extent by the whites and are practiced today in all parts of the country. It is a highly controversial topic, partly because of the many types of jazz and because early varieties were not recorded and are hardly known today at all. Some adherents advocate its derivation from European art music; others consider it essentially African. Rudi Blesh is one of the latter group. He has tried to show that in the beginning New Orleans jazz was African, and that the African elements gradually deteriorated in Chicago and New York.[16] He believes that the following traits in New Orleans jazz are particularly African: microtonal flattening of the third and seventh scale-steps because of the nontempered scales of African music, hot rhythm, individual improvisation, peculiar methods of tone production, and, of course, tendencies to antiphonal technique. These traits are traceable, often indirectly, to African material, although they had assumed somewhat different forms in New Orleans jazz, and Blesh believes that they were replaced in Chicago and New York jazz by other forms closer to European art music. Most important for jazz are hot rhythm, which has been carried in jazz to a greater degree of complexity than elsewhere, and antiphonal renditions of various sections of a piece by different instruments.[17]

We have observed Negro music in its wanderings from Africa to the New World and have seen that certain traits survive while others perish. The greatest degree of survival is found in those areas which are inhabited almost exclusively by Negroes, areas in the West Indies and South America. We have found that the Negro material survives best in European cultures which are organized most favorably for that survival, primarily the Roman Catholic countries. We have found in the English-speaking Bahamas fewer African elements and more inroads of Western techniques than in Haiti, and we have observed in the United States the use of primarily European melodic material with some Africanisms intermingled. We have seen African traits become the main distinguishing features of a style perpetuated largely by the whites and mixed considerably with elements indigenous to Western cultivated music, jazz; we can witness today the great influence of New World Negro styles on modern composers. How can we explain why some of these African traits have survived so long, while others, such as the scales that do not fit into the diatonic system, have disappeared? Waterman has attempted an answer with the theory of syncretism: he states that those traits in African music that are similar to certain features in Western music will survive in a Western environment. Let us introduce also another concept, that of strong versus weak features. A trait that defies acculturation is strong; it will persist in the behavioral conditions of its original cultures and is evidently essential to that culture. Without strong features, the music of the culture would disintegrate; the weak features are expendable. In African Negro music the strong features are antiphonal and responsorial technique and hot rhythm. Polyphony and scale types must be weaker features, since they seem to have been subject to modification. In another acculturated style, Czech folk music, which has in the last two centuries come largely under the influence of German cultivated music, two persistent traits can be defined as strong: a tendency for dynamic contrast in the form of sharp accentuation, and a lack of up-beats or initial unaccented notes. These features cannot be explained, as can those of the New World Negro music, by syncretism, for they have survived in a hostile environment. It is interesting to note that they are similar to Czech linguistic features, namely, stress on the initial syllable and strong contrast between stressed and unstressed units. Thus, approaching the problem of acculturation in terms of strong and weak features may shed some light on cultural aesthetic values, which are difficult to determine from statements by informants. Further study of musical acculturation may give more insight into the problems of acculturation in general and of stylistic change, and, most important because of past difficulties in method, it may lead to greater understanding of the aesthetic preferences of individual peoples.

10

Primitive music in perspective

The classification of primitive music according to geographic areas and the identification of survivals cannot, after all, be divorced from the study of the history of music. Throughout this book we have been intermittently confronted with the questions: How did the present conditions available for our examination come about? What was it that first motivated aboriginal man to sing and to devise his rudimentary musical instruments? Many scholars have dealt with these questions, which perhaps cannot be fully answered on the basis of what we know now, and all their theories have contributed some new insights into the problem of the origin of music. Our task here is to review these theories briefly [1] and to add a new one.

THEORIES ON THE ORIGIN OF MUSIC

The Darwinian hypothesis is one of the earliest. It links the origin of music with sex; music was assumed to have evolved from mating calls, analogous to bird songs and the mating cries of other animals. Man, according to this approach, did not imitate animal calls, but he developed the ability to sing as he did other physical features, prompted by the urge to seek a mate. Advocates of this theory have found some support in the music of birds: albeit bird songs are sexually functional, they may be legitimately called "music" because birds apparently sing sometimes just for the pleasure of singing — there is some organization to their songs that has no strictly physiological basis. Nonetheless, the arguments against the Darwinian hypothesis as applied to the origin of music are many, perhaps the weightiest being the absence of music-like mating calls among apes.

Buecher's theory that rhythm developed first in work songs has already been discussed (see page 62), and the objections to it have been indicated. Stumpf evolved another theory, one which, like Buecher's, lacks pragmatic substantiation. He believed that fixed pitch came into existence from the desire to communicate over long distances, since language can be heard much farther away if it is intoned on one pitch than if it is spoken. In order to validate Stumpf's theory we would have to find sustained monotonic signals in use among primitive peoples today, but such has not been the case. Nadel's hypothesis that music was originally a special means of communicating with the supernatural has also been mentioned before (see page 7). His view appears to be logical, in view of the close connection between music and religion in primitive cultures, but although it does not conflict with any of the other plausible theories, it is supported by little more than circumstantial evidence. The high degree of complexity in many contemporary primitive religious songs discourages assuming that they are survivals of the earliest musical styles.

Although no theories have found universal acceptance, scholars have tended to be most sympathetic towards those that stress the connection of music with language. The view that music originated from "impassioned" speech was held by Jean Jacques Rousseau, Herbert Spencer, and Richard Wagner — who went so far as to use it in justification of a particular musical style. These men believed that when a speaker becomes emotional his speech automatically acquires some musical characteristics, such as fixed pitch, the keeping of a relatively constant vibration rate for a short period of time. Of course, their observations were confined to European peoples and have not yet been either proven or disproven by research among other linguistic families. Critics of this theory have held that the lack of fixed pitch in ordinary speech is an insurmountable barrier to its acceptance, despite the existence of a few musical styles, such as that of the Kubu of Sumatra,[2] that use fixed pitch very little and have continuous gliding instead. Later scholars interested in the connection between music and language advanced the idea that music developed from tone languages, but this met with objections because lexical differentiation according to pitch is a recent innovation in the speech of most regions where it is found (in China and Negro Africa, for example).

My own theory is based on the assumption that an undifferentiated method of communication existed in remote times, one which was neither speech nor music but which possessed the three features that they hold in common: pitch, stress, and duration. Fixed pitch was not present in this early form of communication; durational values were relative and never consistently demarcated; stress patterns were irregular, like prosaic speech today. There was no definite distinction between vowels and consonants. The sounds produced were grunts, cries, wails — things which hardly sound to us like either music or language, but which embodied pitch, stress, and duration. This kind of communication exists today nowhere except in the prespeech noises of infants; and, although the ontogenetic implications of infant prespeech have been examined by Heinz Werner in the realm of music and by Roman Jakobson in linguistics,[3] the study has not progressed far enough to be related to the origins of music and language.

From this early method of communication, whose exact symbolism we cannot speculate on but whose structure we can postulate, the two specific media, language and music, developed. There must have been a long, gradual stage of differentiation and specialization in culture, during which the two became distinct, language taking on vowels and consonants as its chief trait and music taking on fixed pitch. Again, we cannot even guess much about this intermediate stage, but from it arose the existing types of music — of which there are basically very few, despite enormous variegations in detail. This theory, then, postulates three stages in the development of music: (1) undifferentiated communication, (2) differentiation between language and music, with music still in a highly elementary stage, and (3) differentiation between various musical styles. The last stage is, of course, the only one for which we have any data at all, and even that data is fairly recent.

According to this theory, even the simplest primitive styles — those with litany-type forms and ditonic scales — have a long period of development behind them. Certainly "primitive" music as we know it now is a far cry from man's earliest musical experiences, just as the simplest extant cultures cannot be assumed to resemble those of prehistoric times. The dynamics of musical change in a culture is one of the most interesting phases of ethnomusicology and one about which practically nothing has yet been discovered.

RECONSTRUCTING THE HISTORY OF PRIMITIVE MUSIC

How do we go about discovering the musical history of preliterate groups, with no records available for the periods preceding their contact with more advanced cultures? A difficult problem indeed. The most we can expect to accomplish is to demonstrate the existence of historical depth by a small sampling of the developments that we have been able to observe taking place. We cannot hope to unearth enough data to reconstruct the musical history of one culture, much less to describe the entire history of primitive music, in a way even remotely similar to the detailed investigations of Western and Oriental cultivated music. We can only indicate the kinds of change that have occurred in recent times and assume from our knowledge of these that the same developments have been under way for thousands of years.

The following methods have been used to reconstruct the history of music. Not one of them, used in isolation from the others, is completely reliable, but a conclusion verified by a combination of methods may be regarded as relatively valid.

Archeological discoveries of ancient instruments sometimes shed light on musical relationships between separated areas. Of course they cannot give us any clues about styles, since so many possible uses can be made of an instrument; nor can the remains be relied on to give us a complete inventory of instruments for an ancient culture, as most of the instruments we know today are constructed of perishable materials and probably very few old ones survived the ravages of time.

Occasionally native informants can discuss the history of a style or of a group of functional songs. Such discussions are useful and reliable if the material in question is of recent origin. Informants sometimes claim to know from which other tribes they learned particular songs, but information gained thus has proved in some cases to be totally inaccurate.

As we witnessed in the section on music areas in North America, the geographic distribution of musical traits can give some indication of their age and of their origin within the area. Noncontiguous distribution, particularly of a specialized trait, may mean that the trait was possessed by the various cultures during a past era when they were in contact.

Correlation of stylistic diversity and ethnological data may produce valuable information on music history. For example, a certain tribe may have several clear-cut sub-styles within its repertory. From this stylistic variance we deduce that one or more sub-styles were borrowed in the past from other tribes. If we can substantiate this hypothesis by ethnological data, such as known past contact between the tribe and those from whom the borrowing is suspected, it is undoubtedly valid. Most ethnological evidence, in fact, concerns our knowledge of the past contacts between tribes and of the sources from which cultural traits were dispersed, especially cultural traits that involve music. This method is very useful in tracking down the diverse geographic origins of stylistic elements — vocal techniques, forms, scales, rhythmic patterns, etc.

As an example of this combination method, let us sketch briefly a tentative history of Shawnee music in the last three centuries, since this tribe is one of the few that has been examined in an attempt to discover the chronological sequence of songs in the repertory.[4] The Shawnee style is more varied than that of most Indian tribes, and its sub-styles can be correlated with tribal migrations. Originally the Shawnee lived in the eastern United States and belonged to the Algonquian language family, whose members lived mostly on the East Coast, in southeastern Canada, and around the Great Lakes. So far as we know, it was around 1680 that the Shawnee were first introduced to white men, who discovered them inhabiting what is now western North Carolina and Tennessee. Around 1700, some of the tribe were living farther north, near the Delaware River and in eastern Pennsylvania. Thence they moved to Ohio and Indiana in the second half of the eighteenth century, and some of them shortly afterwards moved to Missouri and Texas, where they came in contact with the Southern Plains Indians. The Shawnee who had remained in Ohio subsequently moved to Kansas. So we are sure that the tribe has had cultural contact with other Indians of several culture areas, including the Eastern Woodlands, the southeastern United States, and the Great Plains.

Because of our knowledge of these migrations, we can establish the order in which the four Shawnee sub-styles entered their repertory. The earliest sub-style consists of lullabies and songs from tales; they have small ranges, simple forms, and ditonic or tritonic scales. The style is widespread among many other tribes having songs with the same functions, and it is probably many centuries old. The second sub-style, and the most common, may date from the time of Shawnee contact with tribes of the southeastern United States, whose music closely resembles it. It consists of songs with undulating melodic movement, clear-cut rhythmic units, and ranges of about an octave, and it may have largely replaced an older and more generalized Shawnee style. The next addition to the repertory probably came shortly before 1800, when the Shawnee were in contact with the Plains tribes; it comprises the songs of the Green Corn Dance, which are sung frequently throughout the Plains-Pueblo area. The songs are distinguished by long range, rhythmic complexity, and terrace-type melodic contour. The fourth sub-style consists of the Peyote songs and is indisputably the most recent in origin, as the Shawnee adopted the Peyote cult around 1900. These four groups constitute the contemporary Shawnee repertory. Quite probably, such intertribal musical swapping has been going on for centuries in many primitive areas; the Shawnee are cited here only because of the extraordinary amount of material available on their migrations.

Another method of reconstructing the history of a primitive style can be utilized but rarely: compilation by means of evidence that is primarily musical. The underlying assumption in such an attempt is that simplicity precedes complexity, and this is probably correct in most cases; historical reconstructions whose results agree with this assumption are probably the most reliable ones. Among the various kinds of musical evidence used to trace the history of a style, comparison of songs with diverse functions has proved helpful. Songs that differ in function often differ in style, even though they are all in the repertory of one tribe. Such variance can enable us to trace the origin of a function to another tribe and can thus give us a clue to the age of the functional songs. Some scholars have held the conflicting view that stylistic differences in functional songs are caused by the psychological association of the song with its function in the minds of the natives, and therefore functional songs have not usually been borrowed from other tribes. This theory has been disproven in most cultures, although conceivably it may be true for some others. A third explanation of variance in functional styles has been offered by Helen Roberts,[5] whose study has been of North American Indian music. From a single song that fulfills one function, a number of variants may develop that eventually achieve the reputation of independent songs. They may become so popular that they replace the other songs that have the same function as the parent song but differ from it in style. Such a process may have been responsible for the Yuman and Pima song cycles, which consist of a number of stylistically similar songs connected with a particular myth. The songs of each cycle form a homogeneous group, distinguished by various formulas and similarity of melodic movement and form. Since outside influence was probably not a factor, and psychological explanation must be ruled out on the grounds of indemonstrability, these song cycles probably did develop along the lines that Roberts suggests. However, all such attempts to trace development of a style by means of internal musical evidence are by nature partial and tentative.

Several scholars, notably A. P. Merriam, Richard Waterman, and David McAllester, have studied the acculturation of primitive music as it came under the influence of Western music, over the course of a number of years. They have shown whether or not the various primitive styles have changed, what kinds of changes do occur, and the reasons behind them. Such studies have a vitality and timeliness which are not evident in works that attempt historical reconstruction. Of course, they do not show us what happened under aboriginal conditions: the kinds of things that occur when primitive music feels the impact of a more advanced style are not probably synonymous with those that occur when two Indian styles meet. But the scholars who did the research have been scrupulously careful not to draw unwarranted conclusions.

We have now reached the point where we can utilize our findings about primitive music to try to assign it a place in all the music of mankind, past and present. We have found few essential differences between primitive music and the other types — folk, Oriental, and Western cultivated music. The stylistic differences that do prevail are quantitative rather than qualitative: most of the primitive music is monophonic, while Western cultivated music is mainly harmonic; the forms of primitive music are likely to be much shorter than most cultivated forms, and so on. Every large body of cultivated styles is related by virtue of marked resemblances to one or more primitive styles. Thus it is possible to sketch comprehensive music areas for the whole world, in very broad terms, somewhat as follows.

The world is roughly divided into three very loosely delimited music areas, each of which contains some styles of cultivated music that are obviously its most complex musical forms. In or near the locales that are centers of cultivated music, we also find the related folk styles, which develop along with and interact with the more advanced styles. On the periphery of each area are the primitive styles, which belong to groups of low populations inhabiting large geographic territories. The three groups are distinguished primarily by their prevailing systems of tonal organization, although here again the distinctions must be drawn according to relative frequency of usage rather than differences in kind. The first area consists of Europe and Negro Africa; the music of those regions is related by virtue of isometric materials, diatonic scales, and polyphony based on parallel thirds, fourths, and fifths. The second area extends in a long strip across North Africa, includes the Islamic world, India, and Indonesia, and stretches into Oceania. The use of small intervals in scales, melodies, and polyphony is the outstanding feature of this area. The third and largest area is that inhabited primarily by Mongoloids; it includes the American Indians, the advanced cultures of the Far East, the peoples of eastern and northern Siberia, and even extends into European Russia with the Finno-Ugric peoples. The main characteristic here is the use of large steps in pentatonic and tetratonic scales. These three immense units, within which we find, of course, great stylistic diversity, may have long-standing historical relationships, or they may have developed in relatively recent times, largely under the influence of cultivated music. Division of the world into these units is useful in some ways for classificatory purposes, and it reduces the otherwise endless variety of styles into some semblance of order and simplicity.

Thus we find all three main types of music — folk, primitive, and cultivated — in every large area, each of which has some very simple forms and some of great complexity. The significance of the distribution for our study is this: every nonprimitive musical style is related to one or more primitive styles. Primitive music has played a large part in the history of all music, in both remote and recent times, although this fact is not always appreciated by the participants in cultivated music. Nor, with a few unimportant exceptions, have primitive styles ever been isolated from each other or out of direct or indirect contact with styles of cultivated music, since the latter began to be a professional matter. The world-wide development of music must have been a unified process in which all peoples participated. Hence we find today in scattered areas many similar traits, which could not have originated via any other process and which have been stumbling blocks for those who attempt deep-rooted psychological and physiological explanations of them.

What does this interrelationship between primitive and nonprimitive music imply for contemporary scholars, musicians, and music-lovers? For the musicologist, it means that he cannot study the music of one culture, be it Western European, primitive, or

Oriental, without considering the musical achievements of all the world and fitting his own particular interest into this framework. For the anthropologist interested in primitive music, it means that he cannot go on examining this field in isolation but must, like the musicologist, study his subject in terms of its relationship to other musical phenomena, particularly cultivated music. Present-day composers have already made abundant use of primitive music as a link with that of the West. But the ultimate success of such efforts will depend in part on the degree to which audiences become conscious of primitive sources and recognize their validity.

Annotated Bibliography

The titles given here represent some of the most significant works on primitive music. No attempt is made to be exhaustive, since literally tens of thousands of books and articles would have to be itemized in a complete list. Most of the important areas and peoples and most of the problems are dealt with in the following publications.

WORKS OF GENERAL AND THEORETICAL INTEREST

Abraham, Otto and E. M. von Hornbostel, "Über die Harmonisierbarkeit exotischer Melodien," *Sammelbände der internationalen Musikgesellschaft* (Leipzig), 7:138–141 (1905–1906). A discussion of the problems faced by composers in using Western harmonic techniques in conjunction with non-Western melodies.

———, "Vorschläge für die Transkriptionen exotischer Melodien," *Sammelbände der internationalen Musikgesellschaft*, 11:1–25 (1909–1910). Directions to be followed by the transcriber of non-Western melodies from records to notation.

Bose, Fritz, *Musikalische Völkerkunde* (Freiburg im Breisgau, 1953). The only recent book covering primitive and Oriental music, written primarily for the layman but with many examples and a good bibliography.

Bronson, Bertrand, "Mechanical Help in the Study of Folk Song," *Journal of American Folklore*, vol. 62 (1949). An exposition of the use of International Business Machines for description and classification of individual melodies.

Ellis, Alexander J., "On the Musical Scales of the Various Nations," *Journal of the Society of Arts*, vol. 33 (1885). An early exposition of scale types, including primarily pentatonic and diatonic ones, throughout the world; the cent system of measuring pitch is introduced.

Ferand, Ernst Th., "The Howling in Seconds of the Lombards," *Musical Quarterly*, 25:313–324 (1939). A survey of singing in parallel seconds in folk, primitive, and possibly Western cultivated music.

Fewkes, J. W., "On the Use of the Phonograph among the Zuni Indians," *American Naturalist*, 24:687–691 (1890). A report on and plea for the recording of Indian music by phonograph as the best method of preserving it.

Haydon, Glen, *Introduction to Musicology* (New York, 1941). Chapter 7 of this general work is devoted to a summary of the history, methods, and findings of ethnomusicology. It is good for student reading.

Heinitz, Wilhelm, *Strukturprobleme in primitiver Musik* (Hamburg, 1931). An examination of primitive music in general, and of some styles especially, in the light of basic structural principles such as tension-relaxation; and an attempt to differentiate on a structural basis between cultivated and primitive music as a whole.

Hornbostel, "Arbeit und Musik," *Zeitschrift der internationalen Musikgesellschaft* (Leipzig), 13:341–350 (1911). A critique of Bücher's theory of work as the basis of rhythm, and a survey of the relationship between rhythm and work.

———, "Das Berliner Phonogrammarchiv," *Zeitschrift für vergleichende Musikwissenschaft* (Berlin), 1:40–44 (1933). A history and survey of the contents of the Berlin archive.

———, "Melodie und Skala," *Jahrbuch der Musikbibliothek Peters* (Leipzig), 19:11–23 (1913). The relationships between melody and scale, tetrachords, pentachords, and other intervals; the methodology of analyzing scale and melody.

———, "Musikalische Tonsysteme," *Handbuch der Physik* (Berlin, 1927), vol. 8, pp. 425–449. A survey of scale types throughout the world.

———, "Musikpsychologische Bemerkungen über Vogelgesang," *Zeitschrift der internationalen Musikgesellschaft*, 12:117–128 (1911). Musical characteristics of bird song; differences between it and human music.

Idelsohn, A. Z., "Parallelen zwischen gregorianischen und hebräisch-orientalischen Gesangweisen," *Zeitschrift für Musikwissenschaft* (Leipzig), 4:515–524 (1921–1922). This work on cultivated music is significant for the student of primitive music because it is an early application of the method of reconstructing music history by means of the distribution of musical styles in isolated areas.

Kunst, Jaap, *Ethno-Musicology* (The Hague, 1955). A brief history of this field, with a manual of methods and a bibliography of over 2000 items; the latter is the best in existence. Also included are photographs of important ethnomusicologists, mechanical aids, and musical instruments.

Lach, Robert, *Entwicklungsgeschichte der ornamentalen Melopoeie* (Leipzig, 1913). This work traces the development of musical ornaments from originally organic materials; it is very extensive and detailed, covering primitive, folk, and cultivated music.

———, *Die vergleichende Musikwissenschaft, ihre Methoden und Probleme* (Vienna, 1924). A survey of ethnomusicology stressing interdisciplinary problems.

Lachmann, Robert, "Musik der aussereuropäischen Natur-und-Kulturvölker," in Ernst Bücken, ed., *Handbuch der Musikwissenschaft* (Potsdam, 1929). A systematic survey (not geographically organized) of primitive and Oriental music.

———, "Musiksysteme und Musikauffassung," *Zeitschrift für vergleichende Musikwissenschaft*, 3:1–22 (1935). This article advocates the perception of every musical system in its own terms rather than according to a Western standard.

———, "Zur aussereuropäischen Mehrstimmigkeit," *Kongressbericht der Beethoven-Zentenarfeier* (Vienna, 1927). A survey of primitive polyphony with speculations as to its origin.

Merriam, Alan P., "The Use of Music in the Study of a Problem of Acculturation," *American Anthropologist*, 57:28–34 (1955). A comparison of the effects of Western music on Indian and African cultures.

Metfessel, Milton, *Phonophotography in Folk Music* (Chapel Hill, 1928). A study of Negro vocal sound production compared with that of whites.

Nadel, Siegfried, "The Origins of Music," *Musical Quarterly*, 16:-

531–546 (1930). A survey of the theories of the origin of music, introducing the theory of religion and the supernatural.

Nettl, Bruno. "La Musica Folklorica," *Folklore Americas,* 14:15–34 (1954). A survey of folk and primitive music stressing methods or research and bibliography.

Rhodes, Willard, "Acculturation in North American Indian Music" in Sol Tax, ed., *Acculturation in the Americas* (Chicago, 1952). An example of the influence of European music in North America, among the Dakota and Navaho tribes, as manifested particularly in the use of English song texts.

Roberts, Helen H., "Melodic Composition and Scale Foundations in Primitive Music," *American Anthropologist,* 34:79–107 (1932). The interrelationships of melody and scale.

Rousseau, Jean Jacques, *Dictionnaire de Musique* (Paris, 1768). This early work contains some of the first scholarly information on primitive, folk, and Oriental music; and the association of these three types here foreshadows the organization of comparative musicology.

Sachs, Curt, "Die Streichbogenfrage," *Archiv für Musikwissenschaft* (Leipzig), 1:3–9 (1918–1919). An attempt to explain the distributions of plucking and bowing stringed instruments by psychological typology.

———, *Rhythm and Tempo* (New York, 1953). This general book includes a chapter on rhythm in primitive music, treated from the point of view of several theories of rhythm.

———, *The Rise of Music in the Ancient World, East and West* (New York, 1943). The first section of the book is devoted to a general discussion of primitive music from the technical and cultural standpoints.

———, *Die vergleichende Musikwissenschaft in ihren Grundzugen* (Leipzig, 1930). An introduction to ethnomusicology from a systematic rather than geographic point of view.

Schneider, Marius, *Geschichte der Mehrstimmigkeit* (Berlin, 1934), vol. 1. This survey of primitive polyphony has as a special asset transcriptions of over 300 pieces of polyphony.

———, "Die historischen Grundlagen der musikalischen Symbolik," *Musikforschung* (Kassel), 4:113–143 (1951). An attempt to indicate universal laws for musical symbols.

————, *El Origen Musical de los Animales-Simbolos* (Barcelona, 1946). Of special interest are the theoretical parts giving laws of stylistic change dependent on physical typology.

Seeger, Charles, "Systematic Musicology: Viewpoints, Orientations, and Methods," *Journal of the American Musicological Society,* 4:240–248 (1951). The place of ethnomusicology in the field of musicology as a whole is considered, and its historical and descriptive aspects are differentiated.

Stumpf, Carl, *Die Anfänge der Musik* (Leipzig, 1911). A survey of primitive music from a systematic point of view; although superseded by recent information, still one of the best general books in the field.

Szabolcsi, Benedikt, "Über Kulturkreise der musikalischen Ornamentik in Europa," *Zeitschrift für Musikwissenschaft,* 17:65–82 (1935). An application of the *Kulturkreis* principle to European folk and cultivated music.

Tiffin, Joseph, "Phonophotography Apparatus," *The Vibrato,* 1:118–133 (1932). A survey of equipment for the visual recording of sound.

Wallaschek, Richard, *Anfänge der Tonkunst* (Leipzig, 1903). A survey of primitive music from both systematic and geographic points of view, but based on too little material (because of its early date of publication) to be accurate.

Wead, Charles K., *Contribution to the Study of Musical Scales,* Report of the United States National Museum for 1900 (Washington, 1902), pp. 417–463. Recognition of visual rather than aural principles in the construction of many primitive aerophones, especially in regard to the distances between fingerholes.

Werner, Heinz, *Die melodische Erfindung im frühen Kindesalter* (Vienna, 1917). Musical transcriptions of infant musical utterances. Interpretation of them in the ontogenetic principle.

WORKS ON AMERICAN INDIAN MUSIC

Abraham, Otto and E. M. von Hornbostel, "Phonographierte Indianermelodien aus Britisch Columbia" in *Boas Anniversary Volume* (New York, 1906). Analysis and transcription of 44 Thompson River Indian melodies.

Abraham, Peter, "Dance Cycles of Indian Tribes in Central California," paper presented at a meeting of the Midwest Chapter of the American Musicological Society, Chicago, 1951.

Angulo, Jaime de and M. Beclard d'Harcourt, "La Musique des Indiens de la Californie du Nord," *Journal de la Societe des Americanistes* (Paris), 23:189–228 (1931). A brief survey of Shoshone, Paiute, Pomo, Miwok, Yurok, and other styles, with about 20 transcriptions; these are moderately accurate.

Baker, Theodore, *Über die Musik der nordamerikanischen Wilden* (Leipzig, 1882). An early survey, probably the first serious study, of North American Indian music. It includes transcriptions; at least some are accurate.

Barbeau, Marius, "Asiatic Survivals in Indian Songs," *Musical Quarterly*, 20:107–116 (1934). An attempt to compare Northwest Coast and Chinese musical styles on the basis of a few songs, and to trace American Indian styles to the Orient.

———, "Songs of the Northwest," *Musical Quarterly*, 19:101–111 (1933). A brief survey of Indian songs in western Canada, with a few transcriptions.

Boas, Franz, *The Central Eskimo,* Sixth Annual Report of the Bureau of American Ethnology (Washington, 1888). Includes transcriptions of many songs with indications of their cultural context. The transcriptions are moderately accurate; most were made by J. C. Fillmore.

Bose, Fritz, "Die Musik der Uitoto," *Zeitschrift für vergleichende Musikwissenschaft,* 2:1–40, Appendix (1934). A detailed monograph.

Cringan, Alexander T., "Music of the Pagan Iroquois," Archeological Report, 1899, Appendix to Report of the Minister of Education (Toronto, 1899). Includes over 40 songs transcribed rather well, and some comments.

Curtis, Edward S., *The North American Indian,* 20 vols. (Norwood, Mass., 1907–1930). Some of these volumes, especially those on Plains and Northwest Coast tribes, contain transcriptions of songs by J. C. Fillmore, without analysis.

Curtis-Burlin, Natalie, *The Indians' Book* (New York and London, 1907). This volume contains over 100 songs of many tribes, transcribed in the field, with no analysis or English translations of the texts. The transcriptions are useful, although not entirely up to standard.

Densmore, Frances, *Cheyenne and Arapaho Music,* Southwest Museum Papers no. 10 (Los Angeles, 1936). Contains 75 songs.

——, *Chippewa Music,* Bulletin 45 of the Bureau of American Ethnology; and *Chippewa Music II,* Bulletin 53 of the Bureau of American Ethnology (Washington, 1910–1913). Contains 340 songs.

——, *Choctaw Music,* Anthropological Papers, no. 28, from Bulletin 136 of the Bureau of American Ethnology (Washington, 1943). Contains 65 songs.

——, *Mandan and Hidatsa Music,* Bulletin 80 of the Bureau of American Ethnology (Washington, 1923). Contains 110 songs.

——, *Menominee Music,* Bulletin 102 of the Bureau of American Ethnology (Washington, 1932). Contains 140 songs.

——, *Music of the Indians of British Columbia,* Bulletin 136 of the Bureau of American Ethnology (Washington, 1943). Contains 99 songs.

——, *Music of Santo Domingo Pueblo, New Mexico,* Southwest Museum Papers no. 12 (Los Angeles, 1938). Contains 102 songs.

——, *Nootka and Quileute Music,* Bulletin 124 of the Bureau of American Ethnology (Washington, 1939). Contains 210 songs.

——, *Northern Ute Music,* Bulletin 75 of the Bureau of American Ethnology (Washington, 1922). Contains 114 songs.

——, *Papago Music,* Bulletin 90 of the Bureau of American Ethnology (Washington, 1929). Contains 169 songs.

——, *Pawnee Music,* Bulletin 93 of the Bureau of American Ethnology (Washington, 1929). Contains 114 songs.

——, *Teton Sioux Music,* Bulletin 61 of the Bureau of American Ethnology (Washington, 1918). Contains 240 songs.

——, *Yuman and Yaqui Music,* Bulletin 110 of the Bureau of American Ethnology (Washington, 1932). Contains 130 songs.

All of Densmore's studies, whose chief value is in the number of transcribed songs they include, together comprise the majority of materials on North American Indian music published thus far. They also contain useful information on musical instruments, the functions of music, and the personalities of the singers. The transcriptions are accurate but not very detailed, and the rhythmic interpretations of some should be revised. It is possible to check the transcriptions of certain songs against the original recordings, since some of the latter have been issued on a commercial basis by the Library of Congress. The analyses in Densmore's studies are of less value, although the tabulations at the end of each study are useful in some respects; their chief difficulty is that they attempt explanation of the Indian material from a nonfunctional and basically Western theoretical viewpoint.

Estreicher, Zygmunt, "Die Musik der Eskimos," *Anthropos* (Fribourg), 45:659–720 (1950). This broad study attempts to reconstruct the history of Eskimo music on the basis of musical evidence, and to relate it to American Indian and Paleo-Siberian music. It contains over 40 examples.

———, "La Musique des Esquimaux-Caribous," *Bulletin de la Societé Neuchateloise de Georgraphie* (Neuchatel), 54:1–54 (1948). A detailed description of the Caribou Eskimo style, the simplest among the Eskimos, with examples.

Fischer, Erich, "Patagonische Musik," *Anthropos*, vol. 3 (1908). A short study of the music of the Tehuelche, one of the simplest styles in the Americas, with a few transcriptions.

Fletcher, Alice C., *The Hako*, Twenty-second Annual Report of the Bureau of American Ethnology, Part 2 (Washington, 1904). This detailed presentation of an American Indian ceremony includes transcriptions of the songs (by J. C. Fillmore) at the spots in which they occur, thus giving an accurate picture of the function of Indian songs in a ritual.

———, "Music and Musical Instruments" in Frederick Webb Hodge, ed., *Handbook of American Indians North of Mexico*, Part 1 (Washington, 1907). A brief general survey of Indian music as it was known around 1900.

———, *A Study of Omaha Music* (Cambridge, Mass., 1893). This early discussion contains a number of transcriptions made by J. C. Fillmore and harmonized by him according to his theory of latent harmony. The transcriptions are moderately accurate, the discussion not very useful.

Fletcher and Francis LaFlesche, *The Omaha Tribe*, Twenty-seventh Annual Report of the Bureau of American Ethnology (Washington, 1911). Over 100 transcriptions of songs by Fletcher appear at relevant points in the ethnography; there is no musicological discussion.

Garfield, Viola E., Paul S. Wingert, and Marius Barbeau, *The Tsimshian: their Arts and Music*, Publication of the American Ethnological Society no. 18 (New York, 1951). Contains a large section on music by Barbeau, which includes transcriptions of 75 songs and notes on the individual songs, but no general stylistic description.

Gilman, Benjamin Ives, "Hopi Songs," *Journal of American Ethnology and Archeology*, vol. 5 (1908). This long study is primarily of historical interest; it contains a number of transcriptions.

———, "Zuni Melodies," *Journal of American Ethnology and Archeology*, 1:63–91 (1891). Also primarily of historic interest.

Hague, Eleanor, *Latin American Music, Past and Present* (Santa Ana, Cal., 1934). The early chapters of this book give material on the ancient high cultures of Middle America. The writings of early travelers and missionaries on Aztec music are assembled and quoted.

d'Harcourt, R. and M., *La Musique des Incas* (Paris, 1925). This long study contains material from sixteenth-century descriptions of Inca music as well as contemporary Peruvian songs; much information, with illustrations, on instruments is also present.

Herzog, George, "Appendix: Songs" in Thelma Adamson, *Folk Tales of the Coast Salish*, Memoirs of the American Folk-Lore Society no. 27 (1934), pp. 422–430. Transcriptions of a dozen songs with a few notes.

———, "A Comparison of Pueblo and Pima Musical Styles," *Journal of American Folklore*, 49:283–417 (1938). A detailed study with over 70 transcriptions of great merit. Cultural and strictly musical approaches are combined.

———, "Maricopa Music" in Leslie Spier, *Yuman Tribes of the Gila River* (Chicago, 1933). Transcriptions and notes on nine songs.

———, *Music in the Thinking of the American Indian*, Peabody Bulletin (May 1933), offprint, 6 pp. Examples of notions of aesthetics and music criticism among some American Indian tribes, and quotations from statements of informants about music.

————, "Musical Styles in North America," *Proceedings of the twenty-third International Congress of Americanist*, New York, 1928, pp. 455–458. Vocal technique (relaxed or tense) as the main criterion of stylistic differentiation; some general statements about the distribution of these styles.

————, "Plains Ghost Dance and Great Basin Music," *American Anthropologist*, 37:403–419 (1935). An example of historical reconstruction of primitive music with help from ethnohistoric evidence. The Ghost Dance style is traced from the Great Basin to the Plains.

————, "Salish Music" in Marian W. Smith, ed., *Indians of the Urban Northwest* (New York, 1949), pp. 93–110. A survey of Salish music without transcriptions, and comparison of it to Northwest Coast music and to American Indian music as a whole, accompanied by tabulated analysis.

————, "Special Song Types in North American Indian Music," *Zeitschrift für vergleichende Musikwissenschaft*, 3:23–33 (1935). Discussion of songs from tales, love songs, Ghost Dance songs, and gambling songs among the Indians, emphasizing their simplicity and their divergence from general tribal styles.

————, "The Yuman Musical Style," *Journal of American Folklore*, 41:183–231 (1928). Description of the Yuman style, and formal introduction of the Hornbostel methods in an American journal.

Hornbostel, E. M. von, "Musik und Musikinstrumente" in Theodor Koch-Gruenberg, *Vom Roroima zum Orinoko* (Stuttgart, 1923), vol. 3, pp. 397–442. Description of some simple Indian styles in northern Brazil, and some general statements about American Indian music, including racially inherent traits.

Kurath, Gertrude P., "The Tutelo Harvest Rite," *The Scientific Monthly*, 76:153–162 (1953). A description of one ceremony from the point of view of music and dance, correlating these two arts and showing their interrelationships.

McAllester, David P., *Enemy Way Music* (Cambridge, Mass., 1954). A study of the music of one Navaho ceremony. This book is important because it includes a detailed investigation of social and aesthetic values as seen in music.

McAllester, David P., *Peyote Music*, Viking Fund Publications in Anthropology no. 13 (New York, 1949). Detailed description of Peyote music and its cultural background, and 84 transcriptions from various tribes.

Merriam, Alan P., "Flathead Indian Instruments and their Music," *Musical Quarterly*, 37:368–375 (1951). Description of instruments and instrumental music with a few transcriptions.

Mooney, James, *The Ghost-Dance Religion and the Sioux Outbreak of 1890*, Fourteenth Annual Report of the Bureau of American Ethnology, Part 2 (Washington, 1896). Contains over 100 Ghost Dance songs, mainly from the Arapaho, at relevant places in the descriptions of the individual ceremonies, without musicological discussion.

Nettl, Bruno, "The Shawnee Musical Style; Historical Perspective in Primitive Music," *Southwestern Journal of Anthropology*, 9:277–285 (1953). Reconstruction of the recent music history of the Shawnee on the basis of musical and ethnohistorical evidence.

———, "North American Indian Musical Styles," *Journal of American Folklore*, 67:44–56, 297–307, 351–368 (1954). An integrating study showing musical areas and comparison of them with culture areas.

Roberts, Helen H., "Analysis of Picuris Songs" in J. P. Harrington, *Picuris Children's Stories*, Forty-third Annual Report of the Bureau of American Ethnology (Washington, 1928). Analysis and transcription of over 20 songs, with discussion, especially of variants.

———, *Form in Primitive Music* (New York, 1933). Description of Southern Californian songs with 30 transcriptions.

———, "Indian Music of the Southwest," *Natural History*, 27:257–265 (1927). A brief survey of Apache and Pueblo music with a few transcriptions.

———, *Musical Areas in Aboriginal North America*, Yale University Publications in Anthropology no. 12 (New Haven, 1936). An attempt to characterize individual styles and to give their distribution. Instruments are emphasized, vocal areas only briefly outlined.

Roberts and Herman K. Haeberlin, "Some Songs of the Puget Sound Salish," *Journal of American Folklore*, 31:496–520 (1918). Transcription and analysis, with text and function, of a number of songs.

Roberts and Diamond Jenness, *Songs of the Copper Eskimo* (Ottawa, 1925). A detailed study of a fairly complex Eskimo style with musicological and cultural viewpoints, and many transcriptions.

Saindon, J. Emily, "Two Cree Songs from James Bay," *Primitive Man*, 7:6–7 (1934). Transcriptions and brief notes.

Sapir, Edward, "Song Recitative in Paiute Mythology," *Journal of American Folklore*, 23:455–472 (1910). Presentation of a specialized song type, one of the few examples of narrative song in primitive music.

Slotkin, J. S., *Menomini Peyotism* (Philadelphia: American Philosophical Society, 1952). Contains a chapter on Peyote music by David McAllester, with transcription and analysis. Of special interest are the accounts dealing with Peyote music by informants, and their statements about the value and quality of Peyote music.

Speck, Frank G., *Ceremonial Songs of the Creek and Yuchi Indians* (Philadephia, 1911). Contains over 120 songs transcribed by J. D. Sapir, with no musicological analysis. The transcriptions are moderately useful.

————, *Ethnology of the Yuchi Indians* (Philadelphia, 1909). Contains some descriptions of Southeastern polyphony.

————, *Penobscot Man* (Philadelphia, 1940). Contains over 40 transcriptions by J. D. Sapir without analysis, but with good notes on their function.

————, *The Tutelo Spirit Adoption Ceremony* (Harrisburg, 1942). Contains a chapter on Tutelo music, with notes on individual songs, and 24 transcriptions by George Herzog.

Steward, Julian H., *Ethnography of the Owens Valley Paiute*, University of California Publications in American Archeology and Ethnology, vol. 33, no. 3 (Berkeley, 1933). Contains transcriptions of a dozen songs without discussion.

Stumpf, Carl, "Lieder der Bellakula Indianer," *Vierteljahrschrift für Musikwissenschaft* (Leipzig), 2:405–426 (1886). Often considered the first study using accepted methods of ethnomusicology. Transcriptions of nine songs, with discussion and detailed analysis.

Thuren, Hjalmar and William Thalbitzer, *The Eskimo Music* (Copenhagen, 1911). A general survey of Eskimo music by Thuren and a detailed study of Greenland Eskimo songs by Thalbitzer. Of special interest are the tonometric tables of scales and the discussions of the cultural background of the songs.

WORKS ON AFRICAN AND NEW WORLD NEGRO MUSIC

Alvarenga, Oneyda, "A influencia negra na musica brasileira," *Boletin Latino-Americano de Musica* (Montevideo), 6:359–408 (1946). Discussion of Africanisms in Brazilian folk and cultivated music, stressing rhythmic patterns.

Blesh, Rudi, *Shining Trumpets* (New York, 1946). The first chapter gives a table of Africanisms in New Orleans jazz. Throughout the book the author stresses the relationship of jazz to African Negro music.

Brandel, Rose, "Music of the Giants and the Pygmies of the Belgian Congo," *Journal of the American Musicological Society*, 5:16–28 (1952). Transcriptions and analyses of music of the Watusi and the Pygmies, emphasizing rhythmic materials.

Chauvet, Stephen, *La musique nègre* (Paris, 1929). A survey of African Negro music with many illustrations of instruments and methods of playing them, but with little useful stylistic description.

Heinitz, Wilhelm, "Über die Musik der Somali," *Zeitschrift für Musikwissenschaft*, 2:257–263 (1919–1920). A monographic study with good transcriptions and analyses.

Herzog, George, "African Influence on North American Indian Music," *Christian Science Monitor*, Sept. 15, 1939. This traces African influences in the antiphonal songs of some Eastern Indian tribes who had been slaveholders.

Hornbostel, E. M. von, "African Negro Music," *Africa*, vol. 1 (1928). A general characterization of African Negro music, and an attempt to explain its tonal developments by tetrachords and pentachords.

————, "American Negro Songs," *International Review of Missions*, 15:748ff (1926). Review of several publications of Negro folk songs, primarily spirituals, and an attempt to show African and European traits in them.

————, "Die Musik der Pangwe" in G. Tessmann, *Die Pangwe* (Berlin, 1913), vol. 2. A monographic study with over 40 transcriptions and analyses, and general characterizations of African music.

————, "Wanyamwezi-Gesänge," *Anthropos*, vol. 4 (1909). A short description of the style with a few transcriptions.

Hornburg, Friedrich, "Die Musik der Tiv," *Musikforschung*, 1:47–58 (1948). Transcriptions and analysis, with some cultural details, of this small tribe in Nigeria. Only monophonic songs are included, in contrast to most African studies.

————, "Phonographierte afrikanische Mehrstimmigkeit," *Musikforschung*, 3:120–142 (1950). Discussion and transcriptions of polyphonic songs, with special emphasis on tonality and its effect on polyphony.

Jackson, George Pullen, "The Genesis of the Negro Spiritual," *American Mercury*, 26:243–248 (1932). Presentation of the white spirituals as the basis of the Negro spirituals.

————, *White Spirituals of the Southern Uplands* (Chapel Hill, 1933). History of southern folk hymnody, and correlation of some of its hymns with Negro spirituals. As sources, the author uses historical collections from the nineteenth century rather than field recordings and transcriptions.

Johnson, Guy B., "The Negro Spiritual, a Problem in Anthropology," *American Anthropologist*, 33:157–171 (1931). The problem of African survivals in spirituals presented from various points of view.

Jones, A. M., "African Drumming," *Bantu Studies*, vol. 8 (1934). Transcription and analysis of drum polyphony, introducing an electronic method of recording.

————, "The Study of African Musical Rhythm," *Bantu Studies*, vol. 11 (1937). Transcriptions and analyses of rhythmic polyphony, mainly in South Africa.

Kolinski, Miecsyslav, "Part III: Music" in Melville and Frances Herskovits, *Suriname Folklore* (New York, 1936), pp. 491–760. Transcription of over 150 songs, and description of their style. Characterization of West African Negro music and an attempt to trace it to the Surinam material.

Nadel, Siegfried, *Marimba-Musik* (Vienna, 1931). Transcriptions and analyses of xylophone pieces, monophonic and polyphonic, and distribution of xylophone types in Negro Africa.

Merriam, Alan P., "African Music Reexamined in the Light of New Materials from the Belgian Congo and Ruanda-Urundi," *Zaire*, 7:245–253 (1953). Includes a survey of general styles in African music.

Nettl, Bruno, "Ibo Songs from Nigeria," *Midwest Folklore*, 3:237–243 (1953). Some songs of European origin performed in African style.

Ortiz, Fernando, "La Musica Sagrada de los Negros Yoruba en Cuba," *Estudios Afro-Cubanos*, 2:89–104 (1938). Description of a New World Negro style with many African survivals.

Roberts, Helen H., "Possible Survivals of African Songs in Jamaica," *Musical Quarterly*,12:340–358 (1926). An attempt to trace African influences, and possibly indicate actual African melodies, in Jamaican Negro repertory.

Tracey, Hugh, *Chopi Musicians* (London, 1948). Description of the complex xylophone orchestras of the Chopi of East Africa, and of their poets, composers, conductors, and dancers. Description of composition. techniques but very few transcriptions and musicological analyses.

Waterman, Richard A., "African Influence on American Negro Music" in Sol Tax, ed., *Acculturation in the Americas* (New York, 1952). Syncretism as the main factor in the merging of African and European styles in New World Negro music.

———, " 'Hot' Rhythm in Negro Music," *Journal of the American Musicological Society*, 1:24–37 (1948). An attempt to trace "hot" rhythm through African, American folk, and jazz styles. Transcriptions of West Indian songs and of jazz materials from recordings.

WORKS ON ASIATIC AND OCEANIC MUSIC

Andersen, J. C., *Maori Music* (New Plymouth, N. Z., 1934). A general cultural survey, with a few transcriptions and little musicological discussion, of music on New Zealand.

Bartók, Béla, "Die Volksmusik der Araber von Biskra und Umgebung," *Zeitschrift für Musikwissenschaft*, 2:489–522 (1919–1920). Description of a style of primitive music in the Islamic world, with detailed transcriptions, analyses, and comparative notes.

Burrows, Edwin G., *Native Music of the Tuamotus,* Bishop Museum Bulletin 109 (1933). A brief monograph on all aspects of music with transcriptions.

———, "Polynesian Part-Singing," *Zeitschrift für vergleichende Musikwissenschaft*, 2:69–76 (1934). A survey with examples.

———, *Songs of Uvea and Futuna,* Bishop Museum Bulletin 183 (1945). A monograph on all aspects of vocal music, including musicological, cultural, and linguistic.

Emsheimer, Ernst and others, *The Music of the Mongols* (Stockholm, 1943). Transcription and analysis of about 100 songs, with a general stylistic description.

Hammerich, Angul, "Studien über isländische Musik," *Sammelbände der internationalen Musikgesellschaft*, 1:333–371 (1899–1900). Includes discussion of parallel fifths, whose presence in European folk music is of great interest to the student of primitive music.

Herzog, George, *Die Musik auf Truk, Sonderdruck aus Ergebnisse der Südsee-Expedition* (Hamburg, 1936). Discussion of song types with about 20 transcriptions and analyses of individual songs.

———, *Die Musik der Karolinen-Inseln* (Hamburg, 1936). A monographic study of the materials from the musicological viewpoint with little cultural discussion, accompanied by many transcriptions.

Hornbostel, E. M. von, "Notiz über die Musik der Bewohner von Sud-Neu-Mecklenburg" in E. Stephan and F. Graebner, *Neu-Mechlenburg* (Berlin, 1907). Discussion of musical style and instruments, with seven song transcriptions.

————, "Über die Musik der Kubu" in B. Hagen, *Die Orang-Kubu auf Sumatra* (Frankfurt, 1908). Discussion of style and instruments with over 20 transcriptions.

Hornbostel and Robert Lachmann, "Asiatische Beziehungen zur Berbermusik," *Zeitschrift für vergleichende Musikwissenschaft*, vol. 1 (1933). Similarities between Berber and Siberian music, and tentative historical conclusions, with examples.

Kaufmann, Walter, "Folk-songs of the Gond and Baiga," *Musical Quarterly*, vol. 27 (1941). Discussion of the music and poetry of these primitive tribes in Northern India.

Knosp, Gaston, "Über annamitische Musik," *Sammelbände der internationalen Musikgesellschaft*, 8:137–166 (1906–1907). Discussion of style and instruments with examples.

Kolinski, Miescyslav, "Die Musik der Primitivstämme auf Malaka und ihre Beziehungen zur samoanischen Musik," *Anthropos*, vol. 25 (1930). An excellent comparative study with analysis, transcriptions, and historical conclusions.

Kunst, Jaap, *Music in Flores* (Leiden, 1942). A general study, with tone measurements of interest.

————, *Music in Java*, 2 vols. (The Hague, 1949). This study deals primarily with the art music of Java and emphasizes structure and tuning of instruments as well as historical materials.

————, *A Study on Papuan Music* (Weltevreden, 1931). A good general study with some transcriptions.

Lach, Robert, *Gesänge Russischer Kriegsgefangener*, 11 vols. (Vienna Academy of Sciences, 1918–1952). Contains the following:
Vorläufiger Bericht, 1918.
Vorläufiger Bericht, 1924.
Vol. 1. *Finnisch-ugrische Völker*
    Abt. 1. *Wotjakische, syränische, und permiakische Gesänge*
        2. *Mordwinische Gesänge*
        3. *Tscheremissische Gesänge*
        4. *Tschuwaschische Gesänge*
Vol. 2. *Türk-tatarische Völker*
    Abt. 1. *Türk-tatarische Gesänge*
        2. *Baschkirische Gesänge*

3. *Kasantatarische, mischärische, westsibirisch-tatarische, nogai-tatarische, turkmenische, kirgisische, und tscherkessisch-tatarische Gesänge*

Vol. 3. *Kaukasusvölker*
    Abt. 1. *Georgische Gesänge*
        2. *Mingrelische, abchasische, svanische, und ossetische Gesänge*

This large group of collections contains a total of over 1500 song transcriptions, made accurately but without great detail. The material includes introductions dealing with informants, some characteristics of the music, and comparative remarks, but little cultural background. Lach places the various peoples in their musical environment according to "stage of development" rather than indicating mutual influences. The provenience of these peoples extends from European Russia into western Siberia; some of their music could possibly be considered folk music, and it is certainly related to eastern European folk music. Texts and their translations are also included.

Myers, Charles S., "A Study of Sarawak Music," *Sammelbände der internationalen Musikgesellschaft*, 15:296–307 (1914). A general study with transcriptions.

Roberts, Helen H., *Ancient Hawaiian Music*, Bishop Museum Bulletin 29 (1926). A large study with discussion of all phases of music, including especially instruments with comparative notes, and transcriptions.

Schuenemann, Georg, "Kasantatarische Lieder," *Archiv für Musikwissenschaft*, 1:499–515 (1918–1919). A general descriptive study with transcriptions.

Stumpf, Carl, "Mongolische Gesänge," *Vierteljahrschrift für Musikwissenschaft*, vol. 3 (1887). An early study with good analyses, but transcriptions probably not too reliable.

Szabolcsi, Bence, "Népvàndorláskori elemek a magyad népzenében," *Ethnographia-Népèlet* (Budapest), 45:138–156 (1934). An attempt to trace the music of all Finno-Ugric peoples to a single origin, and to show the similarities between Hungarian and other Finno-Ugric peoples.

Thuren, Hjalmar, "Tanz, Dichtung, und Gesang der Faröern," *Sammelbände der internationalen Musikgesellschaft*, 3:222–269

(1901–1902). A study of an area in European folk music whose styles are evidently archaic and thus have relevance for the study of primitive music.

Väisänen, A. O., "Wogulische und ostjakische Melodien," *Suomalais-Ugrilaisen Seuran Toimituksia* (Helsinki), vol. 73 (1937). A brief description with transcriptions.

van Oolst, P. Joseph, "La musique chez les Mongols des Urdus," *Anthropos*, 10–11:358–396 (1915–1916). A general study of style and instruments, with transcriptions.

Wertheimer, Max, "Musik der Wedda," *Sammelbände der internationalen Musikgesellschaft*, 10:304 (1909). A celebrated study of one of the most primitive styles, with transcriptions, by the eminent psychologist.

WORKS ON MUSICAL INSTRUMENTS

Ankermann, Bernhard, *Die afrikanischen Musikinstrumente* (Berlin, 1901). A survey of African instruments from the *Kulturkreis* point of view, with maps and illustrations.

Dittmer, Kunz, "Zur Enstehung der Kern-Spaltflote," *Zeitschrift für Ethnologie* (Berlin), 75:83–89 (1950). Historical reconstruction of the development of one instrumental type.

Galpin, F. W., "Aztec Influences on American Indian Instruments," *Sammelbände der internationalen Musikgesellschaft*, 4:661–670 (1903). A study of diffusion.

Hornbostel, E. M. von, "Über einige Panpfeifen aus Nordwestbrasilien" in Theodor Koch-Greunberg, *Zwei Jahre unter den Indianern* (Berlin, 1909), vol. 2. A study which presents evidence for cultural connections between Polynesia and South America on the basis of musical discoveries.

Hornbostel and Curt Sachs, "Systematik der Musikinstrumente," *Zeitschrift für Ethnologie*, 46:553–590 (1914). Presentation of a detailed system for classifying all instruments, with description of the types and examples of their distribution.

Izikowitz, Karl Gustav, *Musical and Other Sound Instruments of the South American Indians* (Göteborg, 1935). A detailed study of distributions, both archeological and ethnological, and descriptions of the instrumental types in question, according to the Sachs classification.

Kirby, Sir Percival, *The Musical Instruments of the Native Races of South Africa* (London, 1934). A survey of Bantu, Bushman, and Hottentot instruments with notes on their musical styles and their cultural background; a very detailed and thorough study.

Reinhard, Kurt, "Tonmessungen an fünf ostafrikanischen Klimpern," *Musikforschung*, 4:366–370 (1951). Measurements of the pitch of several sansas in a museum, with the results expressed in cents.

Sachs, Curt, *Geist und Werden der Musikinstrumente* (Berlin, 1929). An attempt to create a scheme for the history of all instruments in accordance with the *Kulturkreis* theory, and distribution tables for many individual instrumental types.

————, *The History of Musical Instruments* (New York, 1940). This includes discussion of primitive instruments and their relationship to cultivated ones.

————, *Real-Lexikon der Musikinstrumente* (Berlin, 1913). A dictionary of instruments, parts, and other related concepts. It is of great value to the student of primitive music because native tribal names of many instruments are included as entries.

Schaeffner, André, *Origine des instruments de musique* (Paris, 1936). A general study, less valuable than Sachs's, including mainly materials on primitive instruments.

Voegelin, Erminie W., "Shawnee Musical Instruments," *American Anthropologist*, 44:463–475 (1941). An example of a monographic study of instruments and their cultural background in an individual tribe.

WORKS INDICATING RELATIONSHIPS BETWEEN PRIMITIVE
MUSIC AND OTHER AREAS OF STUDY

Bücher, Carl, *Arbeit und Rhythmus* (Leipzig, 1896). Ties between economics and music, emphasizing the relationship between work and rhythm, and posing working rhythms as the origins of music.

Driver, Harold and S. H. Riesenberg, *Hoof Rattles and Girls' Puberty Rites in North and South America*, Indiana University Publications in Anthropology and Linguistics, no. 4 (Baltimore, 1950). This study shows the correlation between rattles and puberty rites and thus the relationship between music and culture as a whole.

Herzog, George, "Speech-Melody and Primitive Music," *Musical Quarterly*, 20:452–466 (1934). A study of the effects of speech-melody on musical style, especially in the case of tone languages; collaboration of musicology and linguistics.

Kurath, Gertrude R., "Local Diversity in Iroquois Music and Dance" in William N. Fenton, ed., *Symposium on Local Diversity in Iroquois Culture*, Bulletin 149 of the Bureau of American Ethnology (Washington, 1951). This study shows the problem of local diversity approached from the point of view of music and dance.

Lach, Robert, *Das Konstruktionsprinzip der Wiederholung in Musik, Sprache, und Literatur* (Vienna, 1925). Repetition viewed as a general formal principle in musical and linguistic art forms.

Nettl, Bruno, "Text-Music Relations in Arapaho Songs," *Southwestern Journal of Anthropology*, 10:192–199 (1954). A study of the ways music and words are integrated and how their forms coincide or diverge.

Pike, Kenneth L., *Tone Languages* (Ann Arbor, 1948). A general survey of tone languages, methodology of their study, and special problems in those of Mexican Indians.

Sachs, Curt, *World History of the Dance* (New York, 1937). A systematic and historical survey of dance, with its relationship to music, including a chapter devoted to primitive music alone.

Schuenemann, Georg, "Über die Beziehungen der vergleichenden Musikwissenschaft zur Musikgeschichte," *Archiv für Musikwissenschaft*, 2:175–194 (1919–1920). Relationships between music history and ethnomusicology, and the contributions of the latter to historical musicology.

BIBLIOGRAPHIES AND WORKS OF BIBLIOGRAPHIC INTEREST

Densmore, Frances, "The Study of Indian Music in the Nineteenth Century," *American Anthropologist*, 29:77–86 (1927). A survey of early studies in that field, with some errors, but generally valuable.

Emsheimer, Ernst, "Musikethnographische Bibliographie der nicht-
slavischen Völker Russlands," *Acta Musicologica* (Basel), 15:
34–63 (1943). Contains a generally complete bibliography of
non-Slavic folk and primitive music in Russia, including arrangements of music for piano.

Haywood, Charles, *A Bibliography of North American Folklore and
Folksong* (New York, 1951). A rather complete bibliography
of North American Indian music is included, with recordings
and arrangements. It is organized by culture areas and tribes.

Herzog, George, *Research in Primitive and Folk Music in the United
States*, Bulletin 24 of the American Council of Learned Societies
(Washington, 1936). A survey of the research accomplished to
date, and suggestions for the future. Also included are lists of
field recordings in the United States and their locations, and
selected bibliography.

Merriam, Alan P., *A Bibliography of Jazz* (Philadelphia, 1954). A
very comprehensive bibliography, without annotation but with
detailed indices.

Rhodes, Willard, "North American Indian Music, a Bibliographical
Survey of Anthropological Theory," *Notes*, 10:33–45 (1952).
A survey of important works and viewpoints, what has been
acccomplished, and what yet needs to be done.

Varley, D. H., *African Native Music* (London, 1936). Annotated
bibliography.

Waterman, Richard and others, "Bibliography of Asiatic Musics,"
15 installments, *Notes* (1947–1951). Complete bibliography
of Asiatic primitive and cultivated music, arranged by countries
and cultures, and including a survey of recordings in the United
States.

PERIODICALS DEVOTED LARGELY TO PRIMITIVE MUSIC

Sammelbände für vergleichende Musikwissenschaft, 3 vols. (Munich,
1922–1923). Includes articles by Hornbostel, Stumpf, Abraham, and others on primitive music in vol. 1, which is mostly
reprints from other publications.

Zeitschrift für vergleichende Musikwissenschaft, 3 vols. (Berlin,
1933–1935). Includes several important articles by Hornbostel,
Lachmann, Herzog, and Helen Roberts.

NOTES

CHAPTER 1. INTRODUCTION

1. The most important among these recordings are those of the Ethnic Folkways Library, which is annually issuing albums and long-playing recordings of primitive music throughout the world, and a number of releases of the Library of Congress, which represent primarily some of the materials from the Densmore-Smithsonian collection.

CHAPTER 2. THE ROLE OF MUSIC IN PRIMITIVE CULTURE

1. This is implied, if not stated, in practically all of the general works dealing with primitive music. The assumption that primitive peoples are not able to participate in music and the other arts because they are pre-occupied with more practical pursuits has no basis.

2. George Herzog, "The Yuman Music Style," *Journal of American Folklore*, 41:184 (1928).

3. David P. McAllester, *Peyote Music* (1949), pp. 18–24.

4. Herzog, "Special Song Types in North American Indian Music," *Zeitschrift für vergleichende Musikwissenschaft*, 3:23–33 (1935).

5. Nadel, "The Origins of Music," *Musical Quarterly*, 16:538–542 (1930).

6. Sachs has discussed this topic in several works, all of which are listed in the Bibliography of this volume. Perhaps his most important work on the subject is *Geist und Werden der Musikinstrumente* (1929).

7. *Grimm's Fairy Tales*, translated by Edgar Taylor (Harmondsworth-Middlesex: Penguin Books, 1948), p. 36.

8. Clement M. Doke, *Lamba Folklore* (New York, 1927).

9. Sapir, "Song-Recitative in Paiute Mythology," *Journal of American Folklore*, 23:455–472 (1910).

10. Densmore, *Northern Ute Music* (1922), pp. 202–203.

11. Recorded by the author, 1952.

12. Recorded by Zdenek Salzmann, 1948.

13. Recorded by the author, 1950.

14. From *Music of Equatorial Africa*, Ethnic Folkways Library Album, accompanying notes by Andre Didier.

15. Pike, *Tone Languages* (1948); Herzog; "Drum-Signaling in a West African Tribe," *Word*, 1:217–238 (1945).

16. Harold Courlander, *Haiti Singing* (Chapel Hill, 1939), p. 183.

17. Herzog, *Music in the Thinking of the American Indian*, Peabody Bulletin (May 1933), offprint, pp. 2–3.

18. Tracey, *Chopi Musicians* (1948).

19. Jaap Kunst, "Ein musikologischer Beweis für Kulturzusammenhänge zwischen Indonesien — vermutlich Java — und Zentralafrika," *Anthropos*, 31:131–140 (1936).

20. Hjalmar Thuren and William Thalbitzer, *The Eskimo Music* (1911), pp. 54–55 *et passim*.

21. Barry coined the term in his article "Communal Re-Creation," *Bulletin of the Folk-Song Society of the Northeast*, no. 5 (1933), pp. 4–6.

22. Herzog, *Music in the Thinking of the American Indian*, p. 4.

23. Herzog, "Salish Music" in Marian W. Smith, ed., *Indians of the Urban Northwest* (1949), p. 107.

24. Recorded by Salzmann, 1948.

25. Paul Radin, *Crashing Thunder* (New York and London, 1926).

26. Herzog, *Music in the Thinking of the American Indian*, p. 3.

27. Weston LaBarre, *The Peyote Cult* (New Haven, 1938), *passim*.

28. The informant was William Shakespeare, with whom I talked during the summer of 1952 through the courtesy of the Linguistic Institute of Indiana University.

29. Herzog, "Canon in West African Xylophone Melodies," *Journal of the American Musicological Society*, 2:196–197 (1949).

30. This point must be strongly stated because, although it is obvious to anthropologists, musicologists often act in ignorance of it.

31. McAllester in Slotkin, *Menomini Peyotism* (1952).

32. Herzog, *Music in the Thinking of the American Indian*, p. 3.

33. Vedda song text, quoted in Sachs, *The Rise of Music in the Ancient World, East and West* (1943), p. 33.

34. McAllester, *Peyote Music*, pp. 94–98.

35. *x* is the phonetic symbol for the unvoiced velar fricative, an example of which is the German *ch*.

36. *Peyote Music*, p. 79.

37. Recorded by Salzmann, 1948.

38. These occur in Arapaho and Shawnee Peyote songs that I have recorded. For a fuller description, see my article "Observations on Meaningless Peyote Song Texts," *Journal of American Folklore*, 66:161–164 (1953).

39. For further information, see Herzog, "Speech-Melody and Primitive Music," *Musical Quarterly*, 20:452–466 (1934), a discussion of Jabo and Navaho music and language, and my "Text-Music Relations in Arapaho Songs," *Southwestern Journal of Anthropology*, 10:192–199 (1954).

CHAPTER 3. THE DEVELOPMENT AND DISCIPLINES OF ETHNOMUSICOLOGY

1. Paul Nettl, *The Story of Dance Music* (New York, 1947), p. 83.

2. Robert Stevenson, *Music in Mexico* (New York, 1953), pp. 52–62.

3. Amiot, *Mémoires sur la musique des Chinois tout anciens que modernes* (Paris, 1776); Jones, "On the Musical Modes of the Hindus" in Ethel Rosenthal, *The Story of Indian Music* (London, 1928) (the first publication of Jones's study was in 1799 and it was written earlier); Kiesewetter, *Geschichte der arabischen Musik* (Leipzig, 1842).

4. "Lieder der Bellakula Indianer," *Vierteljahrschrift für Musikwissenschaft*, 2:405–426 (1886).

5. "On the Musical Scales of Various Nations," *Journal of the Society of Arts*, vol. 33 (March 27, 1885).

6. Hans Hickmann, "Arabische Musik," in F. Blume, ed., *Die Musik in Geschichte und Gegenwart* (Kassel, 1951), vol. 1, p. 595.

7. See the Bibliography for Hornbostel's most important works. He probably covered a wider range, both geographically and technically, than any scholar since. He wrote and made transcriptions of the music of primitive peoples on every continent. Although most of his articles are based on relatively small samplings of music from each area or tribe, the conclusions he drew have usually been substantiated by subsequent evidence.

8. Hornbostel, "Das Berliner Phonogrammarchiv," *Zeitschrift für vergleichende Musikwissenschaft*, 1:40–45 (1933). This article gives the complete contents of the archives at that time, plus a list of publications based on them.

9. Kolinski's large work on Kwakiutl music is as yet unpublished.

10. Hornbostel and Sachs, "Systematik der Musikinstrumente," *Zeitschrift für Ethnologie*, 46:553–590 (1914).

11. The majority of Bartók's transcriptions are still unpublished, including large Slovak and Romanian collections. His most important publications, besides those listed in the Bibliography, are *Hungarian Folk Music* (London, 1931), and "Volksmusik der Rumänen von Maramures," *Sammelbände für vergleichende Musikwissenschaft*, vol. 2 (Munich, 1924).

12. Sachs, *Die vergleichende Musikwissenschaft in ihren Grundzugen* (1930); Lach, *Die vergleichende Musikwissenschaft, ihre Methoden und Probleme* (1924).

13. "Musik der aussereuropäischen Natur-und-Kulturvölker" in Ernst Bücken, ed., *Handbuch der Musikwissenschaft* (1929).

14. *Über die Musik der nordamerikanischen Wilden* (1882).

15. "The Yuman Musical Style," 41:183–231.

16. Respectively: "Speech-Melody and Primitive Music," *Musical Quarterly*, 20:452–466 (1934); "Drum-Signaling in a West African Tribe," *Word*, 1:217–238 (1945); "Salish Music" in Smith, ed., *Indians of the Urban Northwest*, pp. 93–110; *Music in the Thinking of the American Indian.*

17. *Phonophotography in Folk Music* (1928).

18. Herzog, "Musical Styles in North America," *Proceedings of the Twenty-Third International Congress of Americanists* (1928), pp. 455–458; Roberts, *Musical Areas in Aboriginal North America* (1936); B. Nettl, "Stylistic Variety in North American Indian Music," *Journal of the American Musicological Society*, vol. 6, no. 2 (1953) and *North American Indian Musical Styles* (Philadelphia, 1954); Sachs, *Geist und Werden der Musikinstrumente*; Schneider, *Geschichte der Mehrstimmigkeit*, vol. 1 (*Die Naturvölker*) (1934).

19. "An Analysis of the Iroquois Eagle Dance and Songs" in William N. Fenton, *The Iroquois Eagle Dance, an Offshoot of the Calumet Dance*, Bulletin 156 of the Bureau of American Ethnology (Washington, 1953), pp. 226–306.

20. According to A. L. Kroeber, *Cultural and Natural Areas in Native North America* (Berkeley and Los Angeles, 1947), p. 142.

21. He has written on both primitive and cultivated music in Indonesia. Some of the Javanese material that is admittedly cultivated music is often treated in works on primitive music because of its stylistic and geographic proximity to the preliterate cultures in Indonesia. Kunst's most important works on primitive music are listed in the Bibliography. His most inclusive works on Indonesian cultivated music are *De Toonkunst van Java* (The Hague, 1934) and *De Toonkunst van Bali* (Weltevreden, 1925).

22. "The Use of Music in the Study of a Problem of Acculturation," *American Anthropologist*, 57:28–34 (1955).

23. Metfessel, *Phonophotography in Folk Music.*

24. Jones, "The Study of African Musical Rhythm," *Bantu Studies*, vol. 11 (1937).

25. Densmore, *Chippewa Music* (I), Bulletin 45 of the Bureau of American Ethnology (Washington, 1910); Gilman, "Hopi Songs," *Journal of American Ethnology and Archeology*, vol. 5 (1908).

CHAPTER 4. SCALE AND MELODY

1. This generally accepted point of view has been expressed by Hornbostel in "Melodie und Skala," *Jahrbuch der Musikbibliothek Peters*, 19:11–23 (1913).

2. If those peoples that recognize solo singing as the only possible

kind, such as the Vedda and Yuman tribes, were confronted with singing in octaves they might so differentiate.

3. Others who have speculated along this vein are Herzog ("Song" in Funk and Wagnall's *Standard Dictionary of Folklore and Mythology*, vol. 2, p. 1041) and Sachs (*Rise of Music*, p. 37).

4. Wead, *Contribution to the Study of Musical Scales*, Report of the United States National Museum for 1900 (Washington, 1902), pp. 417–463.

5. Kolinski in Melville and Frances Herskovits, *Suriname Folklore* (1936), p. 518.

6. *World History of the Dance* (1937), pp. 181–206; *Rise of Music*, pp. 40–41.

7. George Peter Murdock, *Our Primitive Contemporaries* (New York, 1934), p. 302.

8. Herzog, *Journal of American Folklore*, 41:190.

9. Herzog, "A Comparison of Pueblo and Pima Musical Styles," *Journal of American Folklore*, 49:290 (1938).

10. Hornbostel, "African Negro Music," *Africa*, vol. 1 (1928).

CHAPTER 5. RHYTHM AND FORM

1. Riemann, *Handbuch der Musikgeschichte* (1904–1913), vol. 1, pt. 2, pp. 32ff.

2. "General Characteristics of Primitive Music," *Bulletin of the American Musicological Society* (October 1943), pp. 23–26.

3. Herzog, "Rhythmic Cadence in Primitive Music," *Bulletin of the American Musicological Society*, 3:19–20 (1939).

4. *Rhythm and Tempo* (1953), p. 38.

5. This scheme is a modification of that presented by Herzog in *Journal of American Folklore*, 49:305.

6. Gennrich, *Grundriss einer Formenlehre des mittelalterlichen Liedes* (Halle, 1932); Lach, *Tscheremissische Gesänge*, p. 14 *et passim*.

7. "Plains Ghost Dance and Great Basin Music," *American Anthropologist*, 37:403–419 (1935).

8. Herzog, *Journal of American Folklore*, 41:190–191.

9. *Tscheremissische Gesänge*, p. 14 *et passim*.

10. Herzog, *Journal of American Folklore*, 41:190–191; Edwin G. Burrows, *Songs of Uvea and Futuna*, Bishop Museum Bulletin 183 (1945).

11. *Ibid.*, p. 101.

CHAPTER 6. POLYPHONY

1. Helmholtz, *On the Sensations of Tone* (New York, 1948), pp. 252–255.

2. Schneider, *Geschichte der Mehrstimmigkeit*, pp. 7–22; Lach, *Georgische Gesänge*, p. 20; Belayev, "The Folk-Music of Georgia," *Musical Quarterly*, 19:417 (1933).

3. Reese, *Music in the Middle Ages* (New York, 1940), p. 249.

4. Ernest Th. Ferand, "The Howling in Seconds of the Lombards," *Musical Quarterly*, 25:313–324 (1939).

CHAPTER 7. MUSICAL INSTRUMENTS

1. *Zeitschrift für Ethnologie*, 46:553.

2. *Ibid.*

3. *Ibid.*

4. *Ibid.*

5. Sachs, *The History of Musical Instruments* (1940).

6. This definition paraphrases Kroeber in *Cultural and Natural Areas of Native North America*.

7. Driver and Riesenberg, *Hoof Rattles and Girls' Puberty Rites in North and South America*.

8. Densmore, *Northern Ute Music*.

9. Herzog in Smith, ed., *Indians of the Urban Northwest*, p. 105.

10. Roberts, *Musical Areas in Aboriginal North America*, p. 16.

11. Karl Gustav Izikowitz, *Musical and Other Sound Instruments of the South American Indians* (1935), pp. 201–206.

12. Driver, "Comparative Ethnology of North America," unpublished manuscript.

13. See note 11 above.

14. Denis-Roosevelt Expedition, *The Belgian Congo Records*, photograph in accompanying booklet.

15. Charles M. Camp, direct communication to the author.

16. This fact has been used to substantiate the theory that sexual symbolism is involved in most musical instruments. For example, Sachs in *A World History of the Dance* considers the hypothesis that the slit in a long drum is universally symbolic of the female organ and that striking the drum represents the sex act (p. 179).

17. Sir Percival Kirby, *The Musical Instruments of the Native Races of South Africa* (1934), p. 73.

18. Camp, "The Musical Bow in Southern Africa," unpublished master's thesis, Indiana University.

19. Kunst, *Anthropos*, 31:131–140.

20. It is in Polynesia that panpipes occur in the greatest variety of forms, as shown by Peter H. Buck (Te Rangi Hiroa) in "Pan-Pipes in Polynesia," *Journal of the Polynesian Society*, 50:173–184 (1941).

21. Hornbostel, "Über einige Panpfeifen aus Nordwestbrasilien" in Koch-Gruenberg, *Zwei Jahre unter den Indianern* (1909), vol. 2.

22. *Handbuch der Musikinstrumentenkunde* (Leipzig, 1920), p. 128, and other works by Sachs.

23. Izikowitz, *Musical and Other Sound Instruments of the South American Indians.*

24. Sachs, *Geist und Werden der Musikinstrumente*, p. 86.

25. Robert S. Rattray, *Ashanti* (Oxford, 1923).

CHAPTER 8. AMERICAN PRIMITIVE MUSIC NORTH OF MEXICO

1. This chapter is an abstract of the writer's doctoral dissertation, accepted by the Graduate School of Indiana University in June 1953.

2. "Musical Styles in North America" in *Proceedings of the Twenty-Third International Congress of Americanists* (1928), pp. 455–458.

3. Herzog in Smith, ed., *Indians of the Urban Northwest*, p. 105.

4. Herzog, *American Anthropologist*, 37:403–419.

5. *Zeitschrift für vergleichende Musikwissenschaft*, 3:23–33.

6. The information on central California was supplied by Peter F. Abraham, whose research results have not been published.

7. Hornbostel in Koch-Gruenberg, *Vom Roroima zum Orinoko*, vol. 3, p. 415.

8. *Journal of American Folklore*, 49:283–417.

9. Erminie W. Voegelin, *Map of North American Indian Languages*, Publication 20 of the American Ethnological Society (Menasha, Wisconsin, 1941).

10. *Cultural and Natural Areas in Native North America*, p. 142.

11. The culture areas presented here are those devised by Clark Wissler, A. L. Kroeber, and Harold E. Driver.

12. Herzog, *Proceedings of the Twenty-Third International Congress of Americanists* (1928), pp. 457–458.

CHAPTER 9. AFRICAN AND NEW WORLD NEGRO MUSIC

1. Kroeber, *Anthropology* (New York, 1948), p. 765.

2. *African Genesis* (New York, 1937).

3. Kolinski in Herskovits, *Suriname Folklore*, p. 518.

4. Paul Nettl, *The Story of Dance Music*, p. 83.

5. See note 3 above.

6. "Problem, Method, and Theory in Afro-American Studies," *Instituto Internacional de Estudios Afroamericanos* (Sao Paolo, 1947), p. 14.

7. " 'Hot' Rhythm in Negro Music," *Journal of the American Musicological Society*, 1:24–37 (1948).

8. *Shining Trumpets* (1946).

9. "African Influence on American Negro Music" in Sol Tax, ed., *Acculturation in the Americas*.

10. Herskovits, *The Myth of the Negro Past*, p. 218.

11. *White Spirituals of the Southern Uplands* (1933); *White and Negro Spirituals* (New York, 1943).

12. "American Negro Songs," *International Review of Missions*, 14: 748ff (1926).

13. Courlander, *Haiti Singing*, pp. 69–85.

14. All sources state that there are three drummers. Unfortunately, the only transcription I could find (Example 57) shows only two.

15. Courlander, p. 183.

16. *Shining Trumpets*, pp. 18–23.

17. For an example of the rhythmic complexity involved in improvising over an originally simple melody, see the transcription of a commercial recording by Benny Goodman made by Richard Waterman, published in his " 'Hot' Rhythm in Negro Music," *Journal of the American Musicological Society*, 1:24–37 (1948).

CHAPTER 10. PRIMITIVE MUSIC IN PERSPECTIVE

1. For other surveys of the theories on music history, see Nadel, *Musical Quarterly*, 16:531–538, and Karl Nef, *An Outline of the History of Music* (New York, 1935), pp. 3–4.

2. Hornbostel, "Über die Musik der Kubu" in B. Hagen, *Die Orang-Kubu auf Sumatra* (1908).

3. Werner, *Die melodische Erfinding im frühen Kindesalter* (1917); Jakobson, *Sprakvetenskapliga Sällskapelts i Uppsala Förhandlingar* (Uppsala, 1940–1942), pp. 1–83.

4. This discussion was first published as "The Shawnee Musical Style: Historical Perspective in Primitive Music" in the *Southwestern Journal of Anthropology*, 9:277–285 (1953). I thank the editors for permission to reproduce it. I am indebted also to Dr. Erminie Voegelin for information concerning Shawnee movements in postcontact times.

5. "The Pattern Phenomenon in Primitive Music," *Zeitschrift für vergleichende Musikwissenschaft*, 1:49–52 (1933).

Examples of primitive music

Symbols Commonly Used in Transcribing Primitive Music

This list was presented by Otto Abraham and E. M. von Hornbostel, in "Vorschläge für die Transkriptionen exotischer Melodien," *Sammelbände der internationalen Musikgesellschaft*, 11:1–25 (1909–1910). It was introduced to American ethnomusicologists largely through the publications of George Herzog.

$+$	above a note — approximately a quarter tone higher than written
$-$	above a note — approximately a quarter tone lower than written

These two signs used next to a key signature mean that the modification occurs consistently throughout the song; if they are in parentheses next to a signature, the modification is only occasional.

(♩)	pitch uncertain
⌣♩, ♪	pitch quite indefinite, in the neighborhood of where the stem ends
♪	grace note
♩ ♩	dynamically weak tone
P̃	long pulsating tone without actual breaks
⌢ ♩ ♩	strong tie
⌢⌢ ♩ ♩	glide, glissando
⌢.	above a note — tone slightly longer than noted, the lengthening being no more than half of the value indicated
◡	above a note — tone slightly shorter than noted, but shortened by no more than one-third of the value indicated
≡	major structural subdivision
≡	minor structural subdivision

Example 1: Shona Karanga (Northern Rhodesia) song from a tale

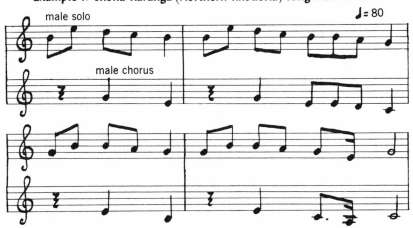

Example 2: Kouyou (French Equatorial Africa) women's dance song

Example 3: Arapaho Peyote song

he ne ne ya   he ne yo we   yo ho ne ne ne   yo ho we

ne ne   yo ho   we ne ne   ya   na na   yo wi na ha ne yo

ya   na na   yo wi na ha ne yo   yo ho ho   yo ho ho

yo wi na   hi yo   wa na   hi ya na   he ne yo we

Example 4: Arapaho Peyote song

♩=120

fine

Example 5: Two Shawnee Peyote songs

♩= 120

Example 6: Shawnee turkey song

tak tak tak

Example 7: Modoc (southern Oregon) song

Example 8: Cheremis children's song

Example 9: Songs with ditonic scales

(a) Shawnee

(b) Vedda

(c) Botocudo

Example 10: Menomini (Wisconsin) song, with its scale

scale:

Example 11: Uitoto song, with its scale (fragment)

etc.

Example 12: Pawnee Ghost Dance song, with its scale

♩ = 96

Example 13: Arapaho Round Dance song

drum: etc.

Example 14: Cheremis song

♩. = 66

Example 15: Arapaho Peyote song

Example 16: Taos Pueblo (New Mexico) song (fragment)

etc.

Example 17: Duma Karanga (Southern Rhodesia) song for musical bow

harmonic voice

fundamental voice

Example 18: Papago (Arizona) flute song

Example 19: Georgian (Caucasus) song

Example 20: Ibo (Nigeria) war song (fragment)

Example 21: Makah (Washington) song

Example 22: Arapaho Peyote song

Example 23: Cheremis song

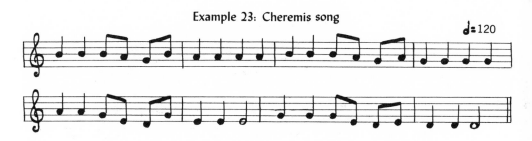

Example 24: Bemba (Rhodesia), music for four drums (fragment)

Example 25: Iroquis (New York) Eagle Dance song

Example 26: Arapaho Ghost Dance song

Example 27: Buriat Mongol song

Example 28: Ibo (Nigeria) children's dance song

Example 29: Arapaho song

Example 30: Arapaho Peyote song

Example 31: Tsimshian (Alaska) song, with its motifs (fragment)

motifs

Example 37: Equatorial African song for voices and musical bow (fragment)

Example 38: Shona Karanga (Northern Rhodesia) song

Example 39: Tonga (Northern Rhodesia) song for voices and musical bow

Example 40: Gur (tribe west of the Caspian Sea) song

Example 41: Caroline Islands song

Example 42: Belgian Congo song (fragment)

male solo

chorus

etc.

Example 43: Caroline Islands song (fragment)

etc.

Example 44: Arapaho song (fragment)

leader

group

etc.

Example 45: Moni (Malacca) song (fragment)

solo

chorus

etc.

Example 46: Uvea (Polynesia) song (fragment)

Example 47: Equatorial African song (fragment)

Example 48: Shona Karanga music for sansa orchestra and voices

Example 49: South African song for musical bow (fragment)

harmonic voice

fundamental voice

etc.

Example 50: Thompson River Indians (British Columbia) song

♩ = 168

drum: ♪ ♪ ♪ ♪ ♪ ♪ ♪ etc.

Example 51: Paiute song

♩ = 160

Example 52: Yuma (Arizona) song

♪ = 228

rise

da capo

Example 53: Navaho gambling song

♩ = 184

Example 54: Choctaw (Mississippi) song

Example 55: Ibo (Nigeria) version of "Frère Jacques" (fragment)

Example 56: "Soleil Malade," Haitian Negro song

Example 57: Haitian drum rhythms from two Vodun cults

Example 58: "Hallie Rock," spiritual (Bahamas)

Example 59: "Round the Bay of Mexico" (Bahamas; fragment)

Example 60: "Another Man Done Gone" (Alabama)

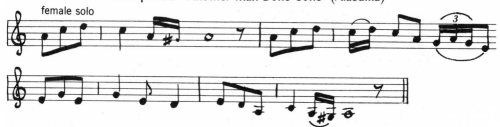

Date Due
